"I warmed both hands before the fire of life..."

Walter Savage Landor

A CHESHIRE GIRL

ISBN 0-9532991-2-0

First Published in 1999 by

Classfern Limited,

720 Borough Road, Prenton, Wirral.

Copyright © Classfern Ltd 1999

Printed & Bound by MFP, Stretford, Manchester.

Front cover; *"On the wide grass verges of the lane, cow parsley burst into a foam of blossom. The oak trees in the hedge threw their shadows across the grass and through the field gates I could see cows and rabbits in the fields on each side."* ..... page 55

iii

The Author

Joan Rocke was born in 1911, one of five children of John William Ivory and Florence Nightingale Ivory.

Her mother's grandfather, Benjamin Delacour, was a painter who had fled France to live in London to escape the persecution of the Huguenots. His daughter, Isobel, Joan's grandmother, married a Walter Smith and moved to America where Walter founded the first teaching Art School in the USA in Boston, Massachusetts.

When Joan's mother, Florence Nightingale Smith, was 18, the family returned to settle in Grassington in Yorkshire, where she subsequently met and married John William Ivory. John worked for a firm of oil merchants in Liverpool, where he rose from office-boy, eventually becoming Managing Director.

Joan inherited her great-grandfather's artistic flair and her father's drive and ambition, combining them to good effect in the many facets of her eventful, varied and colourful life.

Joan Rocke has written many short articles, mainly about antiques and local history, for The Deesider, Cheshire Life, The Dalesman, Yorkshire Illustrated, and more recently, the Wirral Journal. Her first book, 'A Wirral Childhood' was written in 1993 at the age of 82.

Joan now lives in peaceful retirement on the rural outskirts of Chester next door to her son, daughter-in-law and family, and adjacent to the big house around which much of her story revolves.

Illustrations

Foreword

Cheshire has bred many great children. They flit across the pages of our history books like the waves that roll across the sands of Dee before the westerly wind. Their names are writ large in the annals of the world - soldiers, explorers, entrepreneurs, businessfolk, aristocrats - and their deeds and exploits will long be remembered by generations of the new millennium. But it is, perhaps, the less well-known men and women who have made - and continue to make - our counties the rich and colourful places that they are today: those ordinary folk who play their no less important part in the everyday comings and goings of town, village and countryside. And Joan Rocke is just such a woman. I first came to know Joan in the early days of publishing the Wirral Journal, when it was taking its first tottering steps of childhood. I knew what kind of articles I needed, but was not quite sure where to turn. Then along came Joan with just the kind of approach I was looking for. She could write about almost anything and everything to do with Cheshire - and made it appeal to a readership as wide as the Journal's. And, with every article, came the 'icing on the cake' - every editor's dream - photos to illustrate the piece!

Joan went on to contribute to the Journal for many years, and during that time we came to know each other as friends; but I never really got to know Joan's life-story until she published 'A Wirral Childhood' a few years ago. I read those pages with fascination, and hoped she would find the time in her always-busy life to continue the story. And here it is. In some ways, Joan's story is everyman's story: a life full of hopes and fears, achievements and losses, laughter and sadness. But in many ways hers, like each of our life-stories, is a unique story: one that has never been written before, and never will be again. Through these pages I have got to know Joan a little better than I knew her before. Her story reminds me - reminds each one of us - of our self-worth; that we all have a story worth telling, and that every life contributes something to the richness and beauty of our generation. Thank you, Joan - truly one of Cheshire's great children ' for sharing it with us.

Kenneth Burnley, founding Editor, The Wirral Journal, Sept 1999

A CHESHIRE GIRL

To my daughter Vicki, without whose help this book would never have been written.

"A large house could be seen hidden behind the high wall, which was topped with an overlapping larch fence. We could see a few gables and clusters of chimneys, but the overhanging holly and beech trees which blocked our view only added fuel to our already inquisitive minds....."

'Harlow' in Tarvin Road, Littleton, near Chester, later to be renamed 'Hollinsclose' after Joan Rocke's mother's birthplace, Hollinsclose Hall in Bradford.

A CHESHIRE GIRL

by Joan Rocke

CHAPTER 1

It was with a mounting sense of anticipation that we craned our necks out of the car windows. As we turned into Tarvin Road we shrieked, *"There they are - there's the house with the trees with the corsets on"*. - with such an expression of excitement as if we were seeing them for the first time. The old trees grew through the pavement beside the road outside a garden wall in which a gateway gave access to a drive. The trunks were surrounded by white palings held together with wire and, whenever Mother drove us down that road outside Chester, we had to look to see if they were still there, like old friends.

The trees were very tall, a mixture of beech and sycamore and they spread right across the pavement which was about twelve feet wide. As there was no street lighting, the palings were no doubt very necessary to warn pedestrians at night, as the trees were planted in no set pattern, having been originally in private gardens before the road had been widened. On the other side of the road was a long narrow wood full of bluebells and snowdrops in spring and, as the drives from the houses sloped steeply down to the road from each side, one could imagine that the present road followed the course of an old lane through a wood many years ago.

Between the trees in the pavement were long bands of grass which added a rural atmosphere to the area barely a mile from the city centre. Squirrels hopped about in the branches, leaping like monkeys from tree to tree and scattering shells of beech masts everywhere. A large house could be seen hidden behind the high brick wall, which was topped with an overlapping larch fence. We could see a few gables and clusters of chimneys, but the overhanging holly and beech trees which blocked our view only added fuel to our already inquisitive minds.

The weekly trips between term time into the Cheshire countryside were eagerly awaited. We lived in a residential area of Wirral in a large Victorian house but, owing to Mother's interest in all old buildings, we often ended up by having tea in many an old farm house or ancient hall. Her enthusiasm was boundless and infectious and instilled in all of us an acute awareness of our surroundings. Although at this time I was only about 12 years old my capacity for enjoyment, too, was boundless. With my sisters and brother we explored fields, hedges, old quarries, barns and empty farmhouses. We particularly enjoyed spotting the little white fishermens' cottages with grassy tracks leading to the shore of the Dee. We got to know every lane in Wirral where we could expect to find primroses, wild violets, cowslips, blackberries and mushrooms.

Walking out across the marshes at Parkgate with bare feet and wearing shorts and carrying a biscuit box padded with grass, we collected sea birds' eggs and bathed in the sandy channels. The screaming and dive-bombing of the angry gulls added enormously to our enjoyment of the risk we might be taking of being cut off by the reputed speed of the notoriously treacherous incoming tide.

CHAPTER 1

Whilst tea was being prepared in the dining room or kitchen of an old farm house, we left Mother talking to the farmer's wife and went off to explore the farm buildings. Built of hand made bricks, rosy and mellow in the sunlight, the mortar dark and crumbling with age, their colours ranged from pink to coral and rusty brown to red and crimson and some quite blue with damp. I loved the colour of these old bricks and soon learnt to recognise headers and stretchers, and to this day the construction of old walls still has its fascination.

Every door we went through was like entering an Aladdin's cave. Cobwebs infested the arched beams of the barn roof where, occasionally, I spotted Roman numerals on a joist lit by flashes of muted sunlight through the grimy windows. The smell of cattle and damp hay hung in the air. Sometimes a kindly farm hand took us to see the latest calf or climbed with us to the top of a stack where a little owl had laid her eggs on top of a bale.

In the yard of Burton Hall, outside Chester, we saw the huge base stone of an old cheese press, for we were in a famous cheese county. This stone had a channel cut in it to release the whey. Above, on the wall of the farmhouse, could be seen the rusting remains of the hoist that had held the weight of the top stone. This stone now stands rejected outside the Hall on a patch of grass. We always looked for these presses in any Cheshire farmhouse we visited for they are part of our cheese making history.

The more we explored the old villages of Wirral, the more I wanted to discover the history of the houses and the families who lived in them. Many of the families were Catholics like the Masseys and the Pooles, the Stanleys and the Hockenhulls and priest holes were known to be hidden in the fabric of some of the buildings. In 1923 Mother took us to see Poole Hall. This wonderful Elizabethan mansion was built on the banks above the River Mersey and was in a ruinous state. We crept up a stairway made of solid oak to the chapel next to which was a little dark cell and in another room below the floor a secret hiding place for a priest was concealed.

As the farms and old halls we visited were working farms, the whole of the ground floor rooms was paved with huge stone flags in stark contrast to our carpeted rooms. Here I saw a very different way of life to that which we lived in a Victorian house and I was fascinated and enthralled. The doors were heavy and often studded with nails and many of the rooms were wainscoted with linen-fold panelling and had plastered ceilings decorated with bunches of grapes and leaves.

Passages were endless and had many doors leading into mysterious rooms. I trailed after Mother along these endless corridors, and trail I did, because I did not want to miss anything. We came across dairies with huge slate slabs on which the milk was separating in large flat dishes. There were game larders and apple rooms with rows and rows of scented apples on slatted shelves. Large stone pots held eggs in isinglass. Well, we had one of those in our own larder.

Mother and I went every week to Mold Market in Wales where Mother bought a Baker's Dozen of eggs for a shilling. Large quantities of eggs were bought when they were at their cheapest and put down in glazed pottery vessels and covered with isinglass to preserve them for cooking during the winter months when eggs were scarce. Mother and I would set off on Wednesday in the holidays to the market where the farmers' wives sold their wares. We bought chickens and ducks and home grown vegetables each week, for Mother was catering for a large family.

Besides her five children, Mother employed a trained nurse to look after my younger sister, who was very delicate, and a housemaid and cook. All meals were prepared and cooked at home. I could understand the need for the game larders and dairies in these old farmhouses. Although we had no separate rooms we had a cold larder in the cellar with slate slabs all round. Game was hung here and all meat kept cool on the slabs. Bottled fruit and jams were stacked on the shelves and the egg buckets stood on the cold floor.

The room next door to the larder was the laundry, in one corner of which stood a copper. A wooden mangle stood on the stone floor with a wooden trough on each side, one to take the excess water from the mangle and the other for the starch water. A flight of steps from the basement gave access to the garden where sheets and table linen were pegged onto lines supported by stout poles all over the tennis court. Our washerwoman, Mrs Sculley, arrived wearing a boater. Putting on a sacking apron she would set to work to get the boiler alight. The laundry room became full of heat and steam like the engine room of the Mersey. Ferryboats. She had to be sustained all day with large quantities of stout!

The first school I went to was Miss Whiteway's School situated in a large Victorian house on the corner of Stoneby Drive and Mount Road, New Brighton. It was a private school run by two sisters, Miss Mary and Miss Edith. The front entrance to the school on Mount Road was via a sweeping drive with an island of holly bushes opposite the front door. The school stood on a large terrace and at the back of the house the garden sloped down steeply to a tennis court. On the left of the court was a pathway beyond which was a wooded area full of bluebells in spring. I went to the school over eighty years ago and all my sisters and my brother went there at one time or another.

I vividly remember an incident that occurred whilst I was at the school. Playing 'tick' at morning break I careered round the bed of holly bushes in the front drive with my head down and collided with another girl. Our heads met and I remember staggering back feeling quite stunned, but I went back into school and said nothing about it. I did not tell Mother till some days later when she noticed I wasn't eating. Mother took me to a dentist in Rodney Street, Liverpool who discovered I had badly fractured my upper jaw, splinters of which were protruding through my gum and, in doing so, had turned a tooth upside down.

Although I was only four years old when I first went to school we all walked to and from school four times a day as no lunch was provided. Most of the pupils lived locally and these daily walks where we met the other children were a perfect opportunity to make friends. As there was no television we made our own entertainment and were never idle or, more to the point, bored. A day never seemed long enough to execute all our exciting plans; we would happily spend a whole afternoon at the weekend crouching silently amongst gorse bushes surrounding the Oxton Golf Course waiting for a linnet to reveal its nest. Beach combing was another exciting pastime, our most unusual find being a box full of press-studs. Full tins of Brasso were often swept in with the tide having fallen from a ship in the Mersey. Wandering on Bidston Hill one day, we counted how many postholes we could find in the sandstone near the mill where the shipping companies' flag poles had been inserted.

We all loved sketching and painting in watercolour. I specialised in small paintings of wild flowers, but it was my Father who, watching me one day said, *"Get a large piece of paper and a big brush and fling the paint on"*. From then on I started painting landscapes and revelled in the new-found feeling of freedom to express myself. I returned to painting all through my married life, snatching moments when the urge was too strong to resist.

We often went to church in the ancient village of Shotwick. Seated in high backed pews, it was difficult for us to imagine that this now peaceful village once rang to the sound of the marching feet of soldiers who embarked from here to Ireland. It has been recorded that hundreds of years ago one could look down from the Church tower onto a sea of masts. Now the village is but a group of half a dozen cottages on top of a grassy bank. The sea that swept up the harbour is now miles away, the Dee estuary silted up and the land reclaimed; a ring in the churchyard wall is all that remains to remind us of what had been a busy port. The curved grooves cut in the sandstone of the church porch are a visual record of the archers who sharpened their arrowheads before going to the butts on the fields below.

Dad had been a county hockey player and walked with a spring in his step. He had a cold bath every morning and a hot one at night to keep fit and encouraged us to do the same. It was murder. For some years we plunged into the freezing water every morning but eventually we decided enough was enough. However Dad was over seventy before we all persuaded him to give it up.

He had always encouraged us to look, to see, to investigate and to enquire. In so doing he had unwittingly shaped the pattern of my future. It was just as well that he did for it was to stand me in good stead. He loved beautiful things and collected Chinese porcelain, oil paintings and antique furniture seeking advice from Duveen, the well-known antique dealer. He had acquired a small library of illustrated books on antiques, porcelain, glass and pewter and I began taking these books to read in bed at night. Inevitably, I started to poke around antique shops and bought my first piece of porcelain, a Crown Derby blue, white and gold cornucopia vase for 10/- at a shop in Criccieth whilst on holiday and I have it still.

My eldest sister Nora went to Malvern Girls' College when she was thirteen and I followed her two years later in 1924.

After I left school, my parents sent me to a finishing school in Touraine, known as the Garden of France, for a year. They knew my love of flowers and the school had been recommended. Run by Madame Baudoin and her three daughters, the school was accommodated in an old farm house called Le Péré near to the village of Le Membrolle sur Choisille.

The house was stone built and had no upper storey. All the rooms looked out onto a long terrace and the windows were surrounded by the scented lavender blossoms of wisteria. In the garden below was another terrace with a stone-faced pool and steps leading down through a wood to the little river Choisille. Around a courtyard at the rear of the farmhouse was a series of buildings, one of which was our schoolroom. Madonna lilies had been planted all round the courtyard and in the heat of the afternoon the scent was over-powering. Lessons started early in the morning and finished at midday for lunch after which we lay on our beds as it was too hot to go out. Close to the farmhouse were many black cherry trees and we climbed them, when the fruit was ripe, stuffing them into our mouths without restraint.

One day two of us were sent to the farm next door to get some cream. The daughters from this farm, who did all the cooking for Le Péré, wore sabots on their bare feet. To get to the farm we had to walk through a wood of acacia trees whose blossoms were used to make a sweet; dipping the flowers in a batter and frying them till golden brown and dusting the tops with icing sugar. The undergrowth in the wood was a carpet of wild cyclamen.

Chicken was always served cut up into small pieces in a mild creamy sauce. A salad of lettuce tossed in oil and vinegar accompanied this dish. The farmer, who owned acres of vineyards round Le Péré, brought some eels he had caught in the Choisille river as a treat for the English girls. We didn't feel like eating them at first but, stripped of their skins, cut into two inch lengths and cooked like chicken with a rich sauce of cockles on top, they were delicious.

On returning from France I took a course in shorthand and typing and went into Martin's Bank in Liverpool. I had wanted to train as a cartographer but was dissuaded against the seven years training by Dad, who was already supporting my two sisters at art school. The fact was that we were all strongly influenced by the artistic genes of my Grandfather who had founded the first teaching art school at Boston, Massachusetts in America.

Mother had a teaching Diploma and had been a very

successful portrait painter at the age of eighteen. From my Father who was a brilliant mathematician and accountant, we somehow inherited none of these qualities or his wonderful red gold curly hair. From his Irish ancestry we inherited his fighting spirit, a quality he had shown as a young man when, being rejected at his first interview for a job, he turned back from the door saying *"You will be sorry if you don't take me"*. He was accepted and rose to be Managing Director of the firm.

So it was to be shorthand and typing for me and I joined Martins Bank. However I developed a bad attack of quinsy one winter and seemed unable to throw off a temperature. It took some months for me to recover and my doctor advised me to leave the bank and spend as much of my time as possible in outdoor pursuits. As I loved tennis and hockey and climbing in Snowdonia, this was to be no hardship. My sister and I joined the West Kirby Hockey Club and I went out with the Royal Rock Beagles, which hunted in Wirral.

Our childhood was an exceptionally happy one, so much so that, when I was eighty-two, I wrote a book about it called 'A Wirral Childhood'.

CHAPTER 2

I met my future husband, John Rocke, at a picnic on the River Dee. With a group of friends, we had hired a boat from the Groves. As the quietest and prettiest part of the river comes after Eccleston, the boat owners used to take our hired boat as far as the Eccleston landing stage where we were able to embark and load up our picnic. John did not come then but joined the party up-river where we had arranged to meet. I had not met him before and was alerted by someone coming through the bushes behind us. He was tall - 6ft.2ins - and had red gold hair. He was introduced, and I looked into a pair of kindly brown eyes with a friendly expression. We sat down and chatted and later we all went for a swim.

The river was fast moving and deep here so we all dived off an overhanging tree. I did my usual swallow dive, hoping it might draw some attention I expect, which it did. John said he was attracted to me from that moment and afterwards, on the way home, he arranged to meet me again. This was to be a very happy time, getting to know one another, as we found we had so many common interests. It was after a meet of the Royal Rock Beagles that winter down a little country lane near Burton Village that we became engaged. We were married about nine months later at Bidston Church in Wirral on 10th July 1936.

We had rented a little three storey semi-detached Victorian house outside Chester, in Hoole. There were only four houses in our road which ended up in fields and opposite the house were long gardens. The Flookersbrook Stream ran in a culvert beneath the bottom of the road but surfaced again opposite Flookersbrook Hall to run through a small park. John worked in Liverpool in an insurance company and, as there was a sort of back entrance to Chester Station, we were very well placed. He was a member of the Hough Green Tennis Club and we went there most evenings and at the weekends where I was introduced to all his friends. We had a small but pretty garden to the side of the house. A lawn at the front was divided from a paved area by a high stone wall in which an archway over the path was connected to a rockery.

At the back of the paved area was a high wall dividing us from the next garden and against this wall was an enormous pear tree which was laden with blossom every year and, later, weighed down with fruit. Between our road and the main road an access lane ran all the way behind the houses. Here were small coach houses now converted into garages and almost every house had a pear tree so that in early summer the lane was white with scented blossom and bees.

I was able to concentrate on improving the garden which had been sadly neglected when the house was empty. In one corner of a border was a Yucca. This huge shrub, with lance like leaves, like a two edged sword, was reported to flower only once in ten years. During the time we lived there it did flower and rose up like an immense lily of the valley to four feet high and became the focus of interest to everybody who called.

We tackled the garden, digging up and replanting the borders and weeding the rockery. John cut back the overgrown privet hedge and a white rambler rose which had nearly buried the garage. Our garden faced south-west so we paved an area behind the rockery and under the pear tree where we were screened from any passers-by on the road and where, on sunny days, we could eat our meals out of doors. On summer evenings we often cycled into the country taking a picnic, coming home laden with wild flowers which I arranged on an oak chest in the tiny hall. Sometimes our bicycle baskets would be full of blackberries and wild apples.

With the enjoyment of building up our little home we, and our friends, tried to ignore as much as possible the storm clouds which were gathering in Germany and the ominous rise to power of Hitler, whose ruthless and almost manic speeches whipped the people of Germany to the pitch of hysteria and blind loyalty. Our Prime Minister, Neville Chamberlain, arranged a meeting with Hitler in Germany hoping to avert the threat of war. The tension was terrific. On his return, as his plane touched down and the door opened he stood on the top of the steps, a triumphant smile on his lips, waving a piece of paper signed by Hitler in his hand. *"Peace in our time"*, he joyfully announced to everyone's enormous relief.

But it was to be a brief reprieve. All that summer we conducted our lives with as much normality as possible, playing tennis and cycling into the country for quiet picnics, drawing comfort from the summer hedgerows of wild roses and honeysuckle. It added balm to our increasingly heavy hearts. Both of us were hiding our real fears from each other and with the optimism of youth refusing to believe that war would be declared.

One day in May, we sat beneath the pear tree having

our supper, blossom from the tree above floating down like confetti. *"Joannie,"* he said, *"a whole crowd of us from the tennis club have joined the TA at Gilwern, (an army recruitment depot of the Cheshire Regiment) Have you thought what you would do if the worst happens?"* Sick at heart, I had to admit that I hadn't thought at all. He went on, *"Our next door neighbour, Mrs Frost, is to command a local service branch of the Auxiliary Territorial Service (ATS) at the Western Command,"* which stood on the banks above the river Dee in Chester. *"If you were to join this Company you could live at home"*. The realisation that I could live at home and not in billets was certainly a bonus. An alternative, of course, was to apply to Martins Bank for a job. But my mind was made up when a few of my young married friends decided they would prefer to be at the Western Command Headquarters and joined the ATS.

Eventually, about 50 of us met once a week at the Old Drill Hall, where we were shown the rudiments of drilling and were issued with our drab ill-fitting khaki uniforms, their only redeeming feature being their buttons - they were of solid brass and shone like pale gold. As we polished them twice a day, when on duty, they were the envy of the later General Service recruits who had much inferior ones. Tin hats and gas masks were issued and had to be carried at all times.

At last, one day we were summoned to assemble at the Drill Hall and from there we marched, for the first time wearing our uniform, through he streets of Chester to Western Command where we were addressed by Sir Brian Horrocks. It was my birthday, 10th August 1939, when in his final words he said, *"When you are stationed here"*, not, *"**If** you are stationed here"*. My heart sank.

CHAPTER 2

On 3rd September 1939, when my husband and I came down to breakfast, two brown envelopes lay on the mat; they were our calling-up papers. In our Victorian kitchen we had large cupboards from floor to ceiling on each side of the fireplace. I opened one cupboard to take out our breakfast crockery but as I opened the heavy doors a cascade of water poured down onto the floor. The cylinder in the airing cupboard in the spare room above had burst and the water which lay on the large shelves had only been released when I opened the door. As we both had to report for duty there was nothing we could do about it.

When I arrived at the Western Command there seemed to be troops everywhere and we were left standing in the corridors for what seemed like hours. At last, someone came along and I was ordered to open the nearest door. Giving it a timorous knock, I opened the door only to be confronted by a blast of hot air and a ruddy-faced officer in shirt sleeves who yelled, *"Get out!"*. In confusion I quickly shut the door but, in a few minutes, Major Hogg R.E., emerged full of apologies. No woman in uniform had been seen in the Western Command before and to be surprised when improperly dressed was too much! After a little chat I was conducted to a room where I was introduced to Major Barton, with whom I worked for three years, and to two other men.

There was nowhere to sit or even to stand. The floor, chairs and desk were piled high with Bills of Quantities which had to be bundled together and sent to the various Clerks of Works who were hurriedly erecting hutted camps all over the country. It didn't take long to understand what had to be done and we worked like beavers in that first month to make at least some floor space and room to sit down, but as fast as we got them packed up, bundles came in from the Clerks of Works to be checked from a large manual of prices. The quantities of materials needed for each site varied enormously and all nails, bolts, doors, windows, decking boards, roofing felt, manholes and pipes etc had to be assessed and accounted for. This necessitated many visits to sites for measuring-up, which I thoroughly enjoyed, and I became so engrossed in the work that Major Barton suggested I sat for the Quantity Surveyor's exams, which might lead to promotion. I worked hard, passed my first exam and gained my Corporal's stripes.

The doubtful honour of wearing Corporal's stripes was arguable because it came with the responsibility of guard duty at the ATS Billets in Lache Lane, at night. If there had been an air raid warning it was my job to see that all ATS who had evening passes were in by 10.30 pm. Also, to make the awful hot drink loosely called cocoa. To make - take a large white tin jug, empty in a packet of cocoa and a tin of sweetened condensed milk and fill up with boiling water. I had to wait for the "all clear" before I could cycle home, arriving at my house in the early hours. Before I could switch on a light I had first to put up all the blackout screens on the windows. They were composed of a wooden frame on which was stretched black cotton material. I was often very frightened and couldn't wait to get into my bedroom and lock the door.

Soon after the war broke out, however, it was realised that many more ATS were required at the Western Command and about 100 girls were drafted to houses around the town, which were commandeered as billets. These were all General Service ATS who could be posted anywhere in England or abroad, wherever they were most needed. Naturally, they resented the fact that a large number of us were living at home and so we, who had signed up for four years local service, were given the opportunity of changing to General Service or leaving the Army for some other occupation. About 20 of us refused to agree; we had signed for local service and it suited us. So, eventually, a compromise was reached and we were allowed to stay on in that capacity but had to forego any promotion.

Although we had tried to get a plumber to see about replacing our cylinder, we found they were all engaged on war contracts, so John's parents invited us to stay with them. At the top of the old Victorian house we had a very large room, access to which was via an open spiral staircase. It was the worst winter I ever remember. It was so bitterly cold that I slept in my dressing gown and the water in a vase of hyacinths, which John had given me, froze absolutely solid. On each side of the path to the gate, snow was piled six feet high. All day long, huge lorries and army convoys driving through Chester churned the packed snow into ridges two feet high which froze at night. The river Dee was just a sheet of ice hard enough to drive a car over. No able-bodied men were available to clear the roads and these appalling conditions continued all through the first winter of the war. It snowed and it froze, and the heavy guns, tanks, cars and lorries, that ceaselessly drove through the city, aborted the efforts that were made from time to time to chip the ice off the roads, like toffee of a tin.

John and his friends, all Chester men, were billeted around the town and were not allowed to sleep at home. I saw little of him that winter but when they were billeted in a school called the Firs, a mile away, I used to cycle over in the evening taking Mars Bars and was allowed in the Guard room. After about four months John was posted to OCTU, at Shrivenham, Wiltshire. Shortly after I was allowed a week's leave and, as petrol had not yet been rationed, I decided to drive down to see him. In uniform, and armed with my official pass from the Western Command to show to any suspicious military police, I set off in my little Morris 8. By this time all signposts, names of streets, towns and villages had been removed and citizens had been warned, if asked, not to reveal their whereabouts. It was a long journey. Although I had a map concealed under my seat, I took the wrong turning many a time.

Shortly after we were established at the Western Command we were notified that the Princess Royal in her capacity as Colonel-in-Chief was coming to review the troops at the Castle and inspect members of the Auxiliary Territorial Service and the First Aid Nursing Yeomanry. She was to be accompanied on her inspection by General Sir Robert Gordon-Finlayson. As we had never done any real drilling before we were marched to the Castle Parade Ground where a Sergeant Major was ready to put us through our paces. He stood in front of our lines of ATS with our Commanding Officers, Mrs Frost and Mrs Saxon in front.

Suddenly he rapped out an order. None of us moved, so he repeated it with some venom. Mrs Frost looked embarrassed and he marched over and spoke to her. I'm sure she explained to him that none of us understood a word he was saying. Eventually, we were knocked into shape and the great day came. I remember it well; the Princess seemed to have a smile for all of us and the newspaper report said that the division of the ATS and First Aid Nursing Yeomanry (FANY) drawn up for inspection were 'smart on parade and gave the salute with exemplary precision'.

John, now a commissioned Officer, had joined the Cheshires and was stationed at Manchester where he was in charge of a gun site. The huge 303 anti-aircraft gun arrived on a Pickford Trailer and was delivered to the gun emplacement where John and half a dozen soldiers awaited its arrival. John regarded it with dismay as, excepting for brute strength, he had no idea how to get the gun off the trolley onto the gun emplacement. After some abortive attempts the lorry driver strolled across and said, "*Excuse me, Sir, shall I do it for you?*" Used to moving enormous weights he manoeuvred his load as easily as lifting a hen onto its nest.

Manchester and Liverpool were subject to bombing raids every night now and I lay in bed listening to the heavy incessant groan of enemy planes which flew overhead hour after hour and thought of John in Manchester and my parents in Oxton, Birkenhead. My brother John had joined a Cheshire regiment and was serving in North Africa as an anti-tank gunner.

Two of my sisters had joined the WRNS and were stationed at HMS Eaglet (Liver Buildings, Liverpool). They had volunteered to ride motor bikes to deliver signals to the ships in dock. Riding at night in winter with only a tiny strip of light on their headlamps and wet slippery sets on the roads, they fell off more than once. One forgets what it was like to drive in wartime with no streetlights or light from any house or office blocks. Even the ships were in total darkness. The only light came from the searchlights sweeping the skies for enemy aircraft and they, with the anti-aircraft guns and the extremely successful balloon barrage, kept the planes up and off the shipping.

We always knew when a raid was expected because the balloons, which were normally kept on the ground, had disappeared out of sight on their cables, causing an insuperable hazard for low flying aircraft. Unable to bomb their targets, they unloaded their bombs on residential areas, on the return journey, causing many civilian casualties.

Sometimes on summer evenings I would cycle the 18 miles (private cars were not allowed to be driven now) from Chester to Birkenhead, to spend the evening with my parents. Unfortunately, one night, about the time I had to leave for the train to Chester, the air raid sirens went off. Even with a steel helmet it was too dangerous to venture out with flack falling like pieces of jagged metal. About 11 o'clock I cycled down through the silent town to Rock Ferry underground station. It was incredibly eerie but not at all frightening. The blackout was faultless. Not a single slit of light was to be seen in any house. A few Air Raid Wardens gave me a cheery wave in passing. Loading my bike onto the guard's van we raced though the night to Ledsham Station where I was to change trains for Chester.

As I unloaded my bike on the deserted platform the porter said *"Where are you going, luv? There is no train to Chester tonight - because of the air raid it was cancelled, but if it is any help we can take you back to Rock Ferry"*.

I thought for a moment and then said, *"Can you give me time to ring my parents and tell them not to lock up as I am coming back home"*.

The porter agreed and when I came back to the platform the driver of the train called out, *"How would you like to drive in the engine?"* Well, why not, I thought, but I was to experience the most terrifying ride of my life!

20

As there was no need for the driver to stop at any of the underground stations we sped past deserted platforms into what appeared to me, to be a blank wall with only an occasional flash on the line ahead. The driver, chuckling to himself all the time at my reactions, smiled benevolently and opened the door for me to stagger out onto the platform at Rock Ferry.

As the bombing of Birkenhead and Liverpool increased, children were evacuated to Chester and every available bedroom was commandeered. Fortunately, our house was exempt as we were both serving, but later I was persuaded to take the General's A.D.C. and his wife. Somebody had told him that I had an empty bedroom in my house.

Accommodation of this sort was at a premium in Chester with the army stationed there and every hotel filled to capacity. I was summoned to the General's quarters on the top floor of the Western Command. In daytime we did not wear our jackets but were provided with enormous overalls which were all one size. I must have had a dozen safety pins holding it in round my waist, as we were not allowed to wear belts. Thus attired I knocked at the door, was asked to come in, and met Major Thursby. He did not even enquire about the room but begged me to take him and his wife. I told him they could have the spare room and use of my dining room, which looked onto the garden, but that I was not prepared to cook for them. He said that would be no problem as his batman would take care of all that, and so it was settled. They stayed with me for a year and that Christmas when I went into the dining room I saw some very large portraits on the mantelpiece. I recognised them at once, *"Oh"*, I remarked *"these are the Duke and Duchess of Kent's children."* *"Yes"* he said, *"we are their Godparents."*

After they left I had a series of officers and their wives for the rest of the war years. One couple I particularly remember. They were the scriptwriters for the comedian Tommy Handley of ITMA fame. We had a lot of fun together. They read me what they had written to see if I was amused! Sadly, they only stayed with me for a week before he was posted to France. Then John Mansbridge and his wife were billeted with me. His father had founded the WEA. He was an artist and his war job was to paint portraits of all the air aces of the day. He painted the famous Australian fighter pilot, Cobber Kane. Cobber was very young but had made a name for himself shooting down a record number of enemy planes, before he was killed himself.

During the time that Major Thursby and his wife were living with me, we had the worst raids of the war in Chester. For months my sister and I slept on a mattress beneath the kitchen table wearing our tin hats. We couldn't help laughing at each other, we looked so ludicrous.

One very noisy night a frightened despatch rider knocked at the front door enquiring the whereabouts of the A.D.C. who should have been with the General. I knew he was dining at Eaton Hall. The following day Chester was a shambles, glass littered the roads but it could have been worse. Three landmines floating down over the city were blown up by the ack-ack gunfire. There was hardly a shop with a window intact; all along the Rows they had either been blown out or sucked in. Had the mines landed they would have blown the ancient city to pieces.

After two years on gun sites in Manchester during the worst bombing of the war, John was posted to Bombay as a Gunnery Instructor. The Regiment was given leave and sent to a hotel in Southend to await embarkation. I was automatically granted leave to join him. We could see the troop ships out at sea guarded by destroyers. Our time was mostly our own and we went for long walks but were unable to go on the shore which was covered by huge rolls of barbed wire as far as the eye could see.

One morning after breakfast, as we were deciding which way to go, I began to feel decidedly queer as if my insides were collapsing. After walking a short distance we had to return to the hotel. Could it possibly be that I was expecting a baby? We had been married for four years and had been longing for such an event. I discussed my feeling with some of the Officers' wives but, knowing how much I had longed for this to happen, they were fearful of encouraging my hopes. After three days John realised he could not leave me in Southend and obtained permission from his Commanding Officer to take me home but to return the same day. When we arrived at the station every seat was taken. The train was full of troops and a Brigadier and his officers were prowling up and down hopefully looking into every carriage. John summed up the situation, opened one of the carriage doors and said, "*I'm sorry, but could someone give a seat to my wife who is ill?*" They all stood up.

John took me to his parents' home in Chester as I was obviously not fit enough to be at our home on my own. We clung to each other desperately when he had to leave. I had often read of scalding tears and that night I knew what it meant. The tears that streamed down my arms onto my clenched fists burnt like fire. I did not see him again for four years.

The following night I had a threatened miscarriage.

Afraid of standing up I dropped out of the bed onto the floor and crossed the landing to my mother-in-law's bedroom and knocked at the door. A doctor was called, who verified that I must lie still in bed and have only cold drinks. He could not say whether I had lost the baby or not. Two days later, John rang from Southend to say the regiment were embarking that morning. Determined to speak to him I crawled out of bed and dragged myself on my back to the phone in the sitting room.

My sister Pye and Dennis Arkle were married that week at Oxton, Birkenhead. On their way to their honeymoon Pye and Dennis stopped at Chester to see me and presented me with her bridal bouquet. A few days later the doctor decided I was well enough to go by car to stay with my parents at Oxton, so my father-in-law drove me there with great care. However the journey was too much and I started to haemorrhage again. Mother decided to put me to bed in Pye's room, which looked onto the garden and was full of sunshine instead of my old bedroom on the other side of the house. The bed was drawn up to the window and I could look out onto the garden. Our old family doctor was called. He decided to do a 'rabbit test' as he knew how anxious I was not to lose the baby. After a week he returned and to my immense relief and joy confirmed that I was still pregnant but must stay in bed for about six weeks.

During that period my parents entertained Officers who were billeted in houses further down the road and loved to be invited out to spend an evening in a family atmosphere. These young men always come up to my bedroom to have a chat and often brought me bunches of flowers. The most poignant were the Marine Commandos who soon after, at Arnhem, were to lose their lives.

CHAPTER 3

Our son, Martin, was born on 12th November 1942. It was a very difficult birth. About two years later, when on a train to Birkenhead with Martin, I was unable to sit down because of the excruciating pain in the sciatic nerve in my back. My parents called their doctor who arranged for a specialist to see me. He confirmed that I had osteo-arthritis in the sacrum joint, which joins the back to the pelvis. He told me it was essential that my back be immobilised in hospital. This was an unbearable thought and I refused point blank to leave my little son. However, a family conference was arranged with the specialist, who impressed upon me again that, without hospital treatment, I could become permanently disabled.

I realised by now that pleading was to no avail and, because of the intense pain, I could not even sit, but only lie on my tummy. My sister Pye, who had her baby son Bill, volunteered to take Martin and look after him in her home and eventually this was arranged and I was admitted to hospital in Birkenhead. By a stroke of good fortune I had been introduced to a children's nurse who had been commandeered to work in a munition factory.

As soon as I heard I was to be discharged from hospital, albeit encased in plaster, I asked my doctor if the authorities could be persuaded to release her to care for me and Martin at home. Thankfully this was arranged, and so my beloved Alice came to live with us.

In the Times Army Casualty List dated 21st August 1942 my brother's name appeared amongst the seriously wounded in North Africa and stated that he was now in hospital in Cape Town. He was eventually flown home to Alder Hey Hospital in Liverpool which was reserved for troops. Here he had his knee removed and the leg permanently straightened. He was there for nearly a year and was invalided home on crutches looking desperately thin. It was terribly sad to see the pain he had suffered etched on his haggard face. He had been hit in the knee by a piece of shrapnel but it was five days before he and his fellow soldiers had reached hospital by which time septic arthritis had set into the wounds.

The following year Dad decided to take Mother, my sister Pye and her son Billy and me (I was now out of plaster), and Martin and my brother Joni to Criccieth for a holiday. Pye and I were war-weary as both our husbands were in the army in India and we were under considerable strain. We arrived at Chester station with our prams but, as the train was full, we were bundled into the guard's van in almost total darkness which, fortunately, had the effect of sending our children fast asleep.

My brother, who was a very good yachtsman and had often gone out with the life-boat at Criccieth, was greeted by all the locals who couldn't do enough for him. They would carry him down to a boat and take him for a sail. There were a lot of wounded soldiers in wheelchairs on the tennis courts below the house in which we were staying and we used to visit them every day.

One morning, it was 13th August 1945, Joni had gone out to buy a paper. He came back looking very excited saying, *"Everyone is running about saying the war is over"*.

Martin at Criccieth on V. J. Day, 1945

I remember flinging my arms around him and we hugged and cried together in the middle of the road. We all rushed out to hear the wonderful news. It meant so much to us knowing our husbands would be home soon. Later that morning a loud-speaker van drove around Criccieth announcing we could all buy a shilling's worth of fireworks and that bonfires would be lit on Castle Hill and The Green that evening. We queued for ages at one of the shops, everyone talking excitedly to complete strangers as if we had been friends for years - the relief of the tension was so magical.

Determined not to miss the fun, Pye and I tucked our children warmly into their prams and went up to the Green where crowds had gathered. No-one bothered to light the fireworks individually, everyone just threw them into the fire whether they were rip-raps or rockets. The skies were lit up from the blaze on Castle Hill and rockets showered down onto the town. It was V. J. Day and we were all there to celebrate the end of the war, singing and dancing round the bonfire. The joyous ringing of church bells, which had been silent for four years, added to our happiness.

After we returned home it wasn't long before I was notified that John would be arriving sometime on Friday, at the Liverpool docks on a troop ship. As I could not stand there all day with Martin, my father-in-law volunteered to go and meet the ships.

He waited anxiously all day watching every man disembark from every ship as they docked, but John was not amongst them. Disappointed, he rang me about 6 in the evening, but, shortly after, John rang from London airport saying that, as some of them had missed the boats, they were offered an airlift and he would be with me the following afternoon. He said they had had a rough flight as they were literally sitting on one another's knees crammed in like sardines.

John arrived wearing battle dress and our neighbours brought flowers to welcome him home. Of course he had not seen Martin but they soon got to know one another.

It was not so easy for us to adjust after a four year parting, happy as we were to be together again, I was mentally and physically weary. I had had three years of anxiety when John was on a gun site during the worst of the bombing in Manchester and had endured the best part of seven years on rations. My son had been born and for four years I had had the responsibility of bringing him up alone. I had had a spell in hospital and there had been the constant worry of air raids and sleepless nights. My house always had army couples as paying guests all through the war years, which had its problems and compensations but required constant diplomacy and understanding.

John had more than done his bit in Manchester and deserved his posting overseas into comparative safety. Living in the officers' mess they were not rationed and had entrées to all the clubs and race meetings. His every needs were catered for by his batman. Moreover he had a regular job in which he was experienced. He came home to a war-damaged Britain and an Insurance Company that was unable to honour the wartime agreement that he should be reinstated in his old job. Over the war years, as firms had to continue in business, other staff had been taken on. One could hardly blame them for this, but the homecoming troops were kicking their heels with frustration.

At one of the drinks parties given by friends to welcome the men home, John was asked how he was settling down in civvie street. *"It's pretty miserable,"* he replied, *"your place in the firm has been filled and you stand about feeling like a square peg in a round hole. It is seven years since I was in insurance and, as most of the staff have changed, you feel a complete stranger; quite honestly, I don't think they know what to do with us"*.

29

This unsatisfactory state of affairs dragged on for months. John was offered a job in India but the salary wasn't good enough. He found it very difficult to settle down but we were looking forward to our second baby. She was born on 2nd August 1946. The joy of that little girl's birth seemed to pull all the jagged edges of our marriage together. We were a family again.

A friend of ours suggested John might consider joining his firm. It was a high quality manufacturing company and it would be John's job to promote sales and obtain orders from all over the north of England. Fed up with the insurance company, he felt at least he would be his own master and be able to work out of doors, so he accepted.

I didn't think John was very well. Although it was a long time since he had been on the gun sites in Manchester, it must have been an horrific experience to be subjected to heavy bombardment for hours on end week after week and year after year. In every way, noise and violence were anathemas to his gentle and peaceful nature. He was never happier than in a quiet country lane.

So, as soon as the children were older, we reverted, weather permitting, to our evening and weekend picnics. John built a trailer which we could tow behind the Morris 8 and in which we collected enough fallen wood to keep our open fires burning all through the winter months. The smell of it brought back memories of primrose and bluebell woods and later winter berries. I always had bowls full of wild flowers in the house from the country rambles. We brought back mushrooms and blackberries, rose hips and wild gooseberries, which I bottled or made into jam. Once we saw a tree in the middle of a wood covered with small ripe yellow egg plums - we filled our sweaters with them.

I knew John was not really happy in his new job and we were short of money, with two children at private day schools. So I took in a paying guest which was a great help financially.

In the summer John took us to Gower. He had been born at Nicholaston Hall and had spent his childhood there with his parents and brothers. John's parents had owned a large department store in nearby Sawnsea and John and his brothers, Jim and Stan, had a very comfortable upbringing.

Oxwich Bay, which was below their house, was so devoid of holiday-makers that if they saw the mark of a footstep on the sand the boys would look at each other and say, *"I wonder who's been here?"*

They had a hut there, in the trees, in which they kept all their bathing things and the picnic gear. It was never locked. They went from their house to the beach by trap through the lanes. In those days nearly all the Gower was privately owned and only residents were given permission to go on some of the beaches.

As a boy, John had set lobster traps on the headland at Oxwich, so he did the same when we stayed there that summer in a large farmhouse called Parc le Broes. To get to any of the beaches we had to park our car in a farm yard and walk a long way down narrow tracks winding through flower-filled combes. The weather was glorious and we drowned in the heavy scent of honey from acres of pale pink thrift, bladder campion, bell heather, gorse and harebells.

After a day on the golden sands of Slade and

Meuslade beaches, running in and out of the sea and exploring the caves where we were often the only family on the beach, we came home to a hearty farmhouse supper and finished off the day by climbing the Bryn after sunset to watch for glow-worms in the bracken.

John wanted to visit his old Nanny, so we went one sunny morning to look for the cottage. We found it tucked under the side of the hill. It was long, low and whitewashed. John knocked at the door and it was opened by a large elderly woman completely enveloped in a spotless starched white apron. Her face lit up *"Master John"*, she said with delight, *"how good to see you"*. John embraced her and introduced me and the children. *"Come in,"* she beckoned. John ducked his head to get through the low door and we went into the living room.

A fire burnt in the grate and many pieces of copper gleamed on the hearth and mantelpiece. The children sat entranced while she made tea and set the cups on a round table beneath the tiny window, enquiring all the time about Master Jim and Stan and John's parents. The walls, painted white, were about two feet thick and through the tiny window, set into a deep bay with a seat below, was a view of the sea. When we said our thanks and left the cottage Martin said, *"I would like to live there for ever,"* and I think we all felt the same.

CHAPTER 4

My brother Joni, who was now back at work at an estate agent's in Liverpool, was very fond of John and often came to stay with us. They went fishing together and also sailed on the Mersey in Joni's Mersey Mylne, called 'Dolphin' which he kept at Rock Ferry, and competed in races all over England and Scotland.

One day, whilst staying with us, he was taken ill with 'flu and to occupy him I decided it would be fun to put a ship in a bottle, something I had always wanted to do. I had picked up at a sale a pair of attractive hand made green wine bottles each with a raised stamped crest on the top. They were 9½ inches long, 2 inches wide and 2 inches deep with a long neck and the opening narrowing into the bottle through which we had to pass boat, sails and all vegetation. Joni made the tiny boat and sails and I collected twigs and grasses from the garden for the reeds.

When it was all finished I decided to write it all down and send the article to a magazine. Little did I realise the significance of this. To my delight the article was published and I was paid the princely sum of £16.

John used our large Victorian kitchen as his office. There was always a good fire in the grate but I found this behaviour exasperating. This was no way to make contact with possible buyers. How could he make any sales if he didn't go out? To make matters worse, my father-in-law, long ago retired, often called in the morning and the two men would chat and drink coffee together.

This state of affairs could not continue and I tackled him about it one morning as I was beginning to be afraid that he would lose his job, *"Why are you not at the works?"* I queried. He had an office there and surely he and his boss would have discussed which firm or hotelier John was to visit each day. There were also the orders to be delivered. Anyway, wherever he intended going, he needed an early start to load his samples at the works. When I begged him to get off to work he always had some vague excuse, passing it off by saying, *"No-one wanted to do business much before twelve"*. *"But darling,"* I said, *"you have to GET there."*

His indecision was getting on my nerves. A typical incident happened when he had an appointment to see his dentist. The bus left at 10 o'clock from the top of our short road for Chester. The more I tried to hurry him the more he procrastinated until, in the end, at 10 o'clock, he ran up the road. A few minutes later he returned. He had stumbled and fallen and torn his best trousers. He looked very sheepish and crest-fallen so it was difficult to admonish him.

John was paid a monthly salary and very often was made to wait two months before he was paid. As we only had a small private income supplemented by the money from the paying guest, this became a source of worry and humiliation to us both.

I began to realise that his real trouble, although he did not mention it to me, was that he was just not cut out to be a salesman and he hated the job. I appealed to my father-in-law, asking his advice. He decided to write to a great friend of his in London who was on the board of directors of the Liverpool, London & Globe Insurance Company. He was only too pleased to help and a meeting was arranged a few months ahead. Sadly, two days before the appointment, he dropped dead from a heart attack.

About a year later, John's boss asked him if he would like to become a partner in the firm. Naturally, this would necessitate raising a large sum of money which we had not got. I think it was just a polite way of asking John to leave the firm. I suppose it was inevitable as he could not have been very satisfactory.

John decided to go back to insurance but was only able to get a salesman's job. Whilst he was job hunting, I began seriously to consider my position. I had to do something to take my mind off my nagging anxiety. I had recently had a hysterectomy and was recuperating. With time on my hands I often poked around junk shops of which there were many around Chester. The city is famous for its antique shops in Watergate Street and, by studying the goods displayed in the windows, I learnt not only the value, but often the make of a piece I was unable to afford to buy.

I had acquired a lot of valuable knowledge from living at home and visiting the old houses with Mother in my childhood. My father was a collector of oil paintings and Chinese porcelain and both my parents had a wonderful eye for colour. I particularly coveted the Donegal carpet on the floor of our large dining room, patterned in a rich mixture of apricot, Delft blue, scarlet and a little emerald green. It was a joy to behold. Oil paintings in heavy gold frames were on the walls of all the downstairs rooms and they did not go unnoticed. We often discussed their merits with our parents who appreciated our interest.

One day I decided to have a look in a junk shop in

Black Diamond Street, Chester, so called because of its proximity to the coaling sheds by the railway. There I bought two oil paintings, which cost me 2/6 each, in which I could see faintly some sailing ships beneath a heavy coating of dark brown varnish. Cleaned up, I thought, they would look attractive on the walls of Martin's bedroom.

When I got home, I carefully washed off the worst of the dust and dirt, using a mild soap on cotton wool. This careful treatment revealed a tiny portion of blue sky in one corner of the canvas. I tried the soap and water treatment again but to no avail. Then I began to think. If I could learn to clean oil paintings properly it would be a valuable source of income, but to whom could I go for advice? Then I remembered Will Penn, a well known local portrait painter. Long ago Dad had bought quite a few of Mr. Penn's oil paintings and he had given Nora, my eldest sister who was attending the art school, some professional advice.

He was now an elderly man, though still taking commissions, and I was a complete stranger and would be asking a favour from him which, in my heart of hearts and upbringing, I felt I had no right to do. He could have had no possible reason to suspect how desperate I felt, nor could I possibly tell him.

He lived in a white painted Georgian house and it took all my courage to walk up the drive to the front door and ring the bell. He answered the door and, looking somewhat perplexed, asked me inside. I told him who I was, mentioning my father's name and giving my maiden name. I was ushered into his large studio where there was a fire burning. At the other end of this room there appeared to be a platform on which stood an easel at which he had been working.

I did not know how to begin. I knew how desperately important the outcome of this visit was to me and that somehow I could not leave this house until I had an answer to my questions. At last I turned towards him, *"Mr. Penn"*, I said, *"I have come to ask if you will teach me how to clean oil paintings and what materials I will need"*.

He looked not only surprised but somewhat annoyed as he turned away from me without answering and went back to his easel, mumbling irritably, *"It would take a lifetime"*.

After a long pause he said, *"What experience have you had and do you realise how much damage you could do to a valuable painting?"* *"Yes, I do"* I replied and continued, *"I have had no experience, but I have painted and sold quite a few watercolours and I think I have inherited some of my Mother's ability as she was, and I think you know, quite an experienced portrait painter herself and"*, I struggled on, *"I would never attempt to clean a valuable painting."*

All this time I was standing by the fire at the other end of the long room feeling embarrassed and unhappy and sensing I was wasting his valuable time. *"I am willing to pay for my lessons"*, I pleaded, but my words seemed to fall on thin air. We must have talked for another quarter of an hour, then the suspense, worry and anxiety began to take' their toll and I could not stop the tears of frustration that began to trickle down my cheeks. I turned and sat down by the fire with my back to him. I was drained. I had nothing more to say. I could hear him painting and then he put down his brush.

Perhaps something of my despair and my forlorn hunched figure and his friendship with my parents made him decide that at least he would make an effort.

He came over to me by the fire and stood behind me. *"You must realise"*, he said kindly, *"that what you are asking me to do is quite impossible. It takes years of practice in painting and you need a knowledge of paints and varnishes and their composition. Many paintings, after the varnish is removed, need careful restoration, as artists' brush strokes vary considerably in the same way as we can be identified by our hand writing"*.

I felt as if I had a great weight inside me, fighting to get out and my legs felt like lead, but I could not give up now. He sat down on a chair at the other side of the fire. *"Well, Joan"*, he said with a tired and slightly amused expression on his face, *"you certainly are determined. If you would like to come to my studio next week, I will give you some advice about removing the old varnish but you are not to divulge it to anyone"*. I thanked him gratefully and this was the start of many visits to his studio.

CHAPTER 5

About this time, following my success with the 'Ship in a Bottle', I decided to try my hand again at writing. With an old typewriter that Dad had leant me from the office, I wrote about the old houses in Wirral and Cheshire of which, in many cases, I literally had inside knowledge, having visited them with Mother. As some of these had since been pulled down, I felt my memories were worth recording.

I wrote about any subject that interested me and there were many. It often meant a visit to the Library or Record Office where I would spend a whole morning researching my subject and making copious notes. I sent my articles to Cheshire Life, Deesider and, later, the Wirral Journal. Of course I had rejections, but I also had many acceptances.

When we were children we stayed every Easter in Grassington with Mother's sister, Auntie Mim, in her 300 year old stone house called 'Ellesmere'. Situated at the top of the village, we reached it through the Slype, a stone passageway beneath the houses. A cobbled right of way crossed in front of her house but Grandmother had this closed. The house looked across the fields to Grass Woods.

Our holidays there were such unadulterated bliss from morning to night that mere words cannot convey the magic of those days. With our cousins we were often the only 'outsiders' in Grassington, but everyone knew who we were. My cousin, Tom Blackburn, owned the local grouse moors where we were free to wander as often as we pleased. We kept to the pathways made by the guns so as not to disturb the grouse. We ran up the steep stony winding track on whose banks the little yellow mountain pansy grew in profusion. We often met the keepers, who doffed their caps and gave us a cheery grin. I wrote about our holidays in Grassington and sent it to The Dalesman where it was published.

A few years after John was discharged from the army, Auntie Mim invited us all to come and stay at Ellesmere. We were delighted as I so much wanted to show John and the children all the places which we had enjoyed on our Easter holidays - The Gaistrells, Linton church where my Grandmother was buried and Mum and Dad had been married, the stepping stones across the River Wharfe over which they had run after their wedding, Kilnsey Craig, at which we threw stones from the road and were never able to hit, Malham Cove, and the smithy at the bottom of the cobbled street at Grassington where we had spent many happy hours.

Then Ellesmere was full of family history. The kitchen, which one entered from the stone porch, was a welcoming place with the fire always lit and the oak rack hanging from the ceiling. I could just picture my Aunt, sitting at the kitchen table beneath the window during the war cleaning the sphagnum moss of twigs which she had collected from the moor. It was used for surgical dressings and when sacks marked 'Ellesmere' arrived at the hospital, the nurses knew they need not examine it further. Always her sacks were perfect.

During the war, too, when all food was scarce, she inadvertently mixed a bag of caraway seeds with a packet of tea. She poured it all onto a newspaper and meticulously

John Rocke

separated the tea and the seeds with a needle.

Tom told John he could fish the Wharfe as he owned the fishing rights on both banks for a considerable distance. I re-lived my childhood memories by showing my children the barns where we played in the hay and the drifts of primroses and wood anemones in Grass Woods.

When we returned home I obtained my first commission. One of my paying guests asked me if I would clean a family portrait, which he would bring back from Scotland on his next visit home.

The painting was very dark and dirty and depicted a man dressed in armour. The canvas really needed re-lining, but I had had no training in this as it is a job for a specialist. Old canvases can become slack and brittle if not properly cared for, and the remedy is to apply a new canvas which is glued with heat onto the back of the old one. The new canvas is then attached to the stretchers, i.e. the frame. However, I did my best by slightly damping the back of the canvas, pulling it gently and re-attaching it to the stretchers.

First I washed the canvas with baby soap and cotton wool. I then proceeded to remove the old varnish as I had been taught. When the old varnish has been removed, cleaning an inch at a time, there are nearly always areas that need retouching and there is nothing more difficult than trying to match skin tones. There is an enormous range from pink, rose, blue, white and yellow to be considered. Shadows beneath the eyes, the cheeks, chin and side of the nose, all make up the face of the individual and its character. I worked a little on the face each day propping the painting on an easel where it got the direct light from my dining room window. Each morning I opened the door and looked at the canvas. If I could see where I had retouched it I worked on it again, until in the end it was invisible. Finally, the new varnish was applied.

I am afraid John's job did not last very long. Every month there was an assessment of completed sales and if this did not come up to the quota immense pressure was put on John to do better. After about six months of this treatment, John just couldn't take any more. He was now coming to bed very late at night. As I went upstairs he would say, *"I'll be up in a minute,"* but the hours dragged by until it was often 2 o'clock in the morning. I was miserably unhappy and often cried myself to sleep. He was still job hunting after a fashion, but although he had a good appetite he looked gaunt. I begged him to see his doctor but he hated the thought of going and made no effort to make an appointment.

My brother Joni, now having his job at the estate agent in Chester, came to me for lunch every day. It was lovely seeing him and if John was at home it cheered him up. I absolutely adored my brother, as indeed we all did. He was the kindest and most affectionate person I have ever known. He delighted in being with the family, always welcoming us with a huge hug. I suppose he had my Mother's colouring, being very fair, but he was small and wiry like my father and full of the blarney. He had many loyal friends, especially his sailing friends, many of whom he had trained to crew for him and with whom he went on wild and wicked trips to Ireland every year.

He had been an officer on the Winston Churchill and the Malcolm Miller, both sail training ships. Though his gammy leg was a hindrance, he had been picked out of hundreds of applicants because of his reliability, knowledge of sailing and high standards in training young people. Joni was such fun to be with, always seeing the funny side of every situation, but also possessing that rare quality of being able to show sympathy and concern when needed.

I suppose one of his finest qualities was his ability to cope without getting in a panic. I think I would rather have been with him than with anyone else in the world in a tight corner. When he was posted overseas during the war we four sisters bought him a silver brandy flask on which our names were engraved. It was the only article he had returned by the War Office from the kitbag he had left in South Africa after he was wounded.

John and I were friendly with the Chapter Clerk at Chester Cathedral. I asked him if he would allow me to clean the huge canvases in the refectory, which depicted the coats of arms of the Norman Earls of Chester. They were very dirty and needed all the old varnish removing. One was 16 feet long and the other two were 8 feet long. The Norman Earls depicted on the larger canvas were Hugh Lupus, Richard de Ranulf, Ranulf the Second, H. Kaviliock, R. Blundeville, John Scott, Edward, son of Edward 3rd, Edward son of Edward 2nd, and George, father of George 3rd. Of the two smaller ones, one depicted the Arms of the Barons of the Court of Hugh Lupus, Archbishop of York, Archbishop of Chester, Haulton, Hawarden, and Nantwich. The other canvas depicted the arms of Malpas, Shipbrook, Dunham, Kinderton and Stockport.

Having agreed a price, we then had to decide where I would be able to work on them in comfort. I was not prepared to clean them at the cathedral and knew I could manage the cleaning of the two 8 foot long canvases at home. Eventually, after ringing round all my friends, I had the offer of a very long garage which could accommodate the sixteen-foot canvas. The army were approached and they lowered the framed canvas down off the refectory wall and loaded it onto a huge trailer. They put bricks beneath the frame to keep it off the floor and it was eventually placed into position and the garage door closed.

I tackled the cleaning sitting on a stool. Sometimes it

was so cold I wore three sweaters. I had to keep the garage doors wide open to get the best possible light and to let out the fumes from the cleaning fluid. It took me many weeks, much longer than the time I took at home on the smaller ones. Then there was the problem of re-varnishing. Both the canvas and the varnish have to be warm to be applied satisfactorily and, ideally, this should be done in a dust free environment. Fortunately, the varnish dries pretty quickly and so I waited until we had a very hot, windless, sunny day and, with friends, lifted the canvas out onto the drive. Only one coat is applied using a special varnish brush and when the varnish is warmed it becomes thin and fluid and spreads easily. I was glad to see the paintings safely returned to the refectory where they hang to this day.

Jimmy McGuinness, Colonel of the 4th Battalion Cheshire Regiment, was a very old friend of ours. He rang one day to tell me he had arranged an appointment with the Commanding Officer at the Castle as he would like me to have a look at some of the regimental portraits etc., which needed cleaning. I was very nervous, as I did not feel confident enough unless I had had time to view the paintings beforehand. So, I decided to get to the Officers' Mess half an hour before my appointment was due with the Colonel.

Fortunately, he arrived late, full of apologies, but it had given me plenty of time to assess the portraits. Over a sherry, we agreed prices and he said he would arrange for some men to deliver two of them to my home. Then he asked me to come and look at a large painting of a battle scene, which hung on the staircase wall. It had been painted over in parts with a brown paint disguising some damage beneath. I could see it was not going to be easy, but I did not want to turn down any work so I told him that as soon as I had restored the portraits he could exchange them with this painting.

When I returned the portraits, the large canvas was duly delivered and taken into the dining room at Kilmorey and propped against the wall. There, in a good light, I was able to assess the damage, which was pretty extensive. Obviously, officers walking down the stairs with their swagger canes hooked beneath their arms, had, in passing, accidentally made holes in the canvas from time to time, which had later been disguised with a thick brown paint, the colour of the old varnish.

It was going to be a difficult, tedious and lengthy job to restore. Joni was staying with me at the time and I showed it to him. *"I don't know where to start"*. I moaned. We stood examining the painting together, intrigued with the jumble of horses and men on the ground. Suddenly he stood up and said, *"Well, Joanie, you can do it and I'll give you a start"*. Before I could stop him he had opened a bottle of the cleaning fluid which stood on a tray on the dining room table and flung it across the painting. *"Now"*, he said, *"you've got to do it"*. How right he was!

CHAPTER 6.

Before Martin was born John and I had decided that if it were a boy we would send him to Sedbergh, even though John was an old Carthusian. We had seen the school when John's brother Stan was there and had fallen in love with the school surroundings as we both loved the mountains. Martin and Vicki were both at private schools, but Martin was due to go to Sedbergh in two years time. It was obvious that our present income would not cover this. John was struggling and I felt the onus fell on me to try and get some kind of part time job, but what? I had had no training excepting my shorthand and typing, but I did not want an office job.

I had always had a lot of patience with little children and had worked with the Invalid Children's Association for many years before I was married, collecting the children by ambulance and taking them to the ICA in Hamilton Square, Birkenhead, for treatment, after which I collected them for the return trip.

I called at the County Council Offices in Chester and asked their advice. They felt they had the perfect job for me as a home tutor and if I would fill in a form they would send it to their Ellesmere Port offices. The questionnaire duly arrived. My name and address and age, where I was educated (at the Birkenhead GPDST High School and then Malvern Girls College) - What experience? I told them of my work with the ICA before I was married and that I now had two children of my own.

About a week later I was asked to report at the Ellesmere Port offices. I told them I only wished to teach children between the ages of 4 and 12.

After a short interview the officer told me what I was to be paid and said that they would be pleased to employ me as a home tutor. I knew that all these children would be either too sick to be taught at school, or too disturbed or disruptive. I was to teach each child for a year, at the end of which I would report to the school on the child's progress. It was arranged that I worked a five day week on the basis of four hours per morning, two hours with each child. They would send me a rota with all names and addresses and ages of the children, but would not mention their physical condition, which was something I had to find out for myself, often the hard way.

I knew little of the modern method of teaching young children but felt I was capable of teaching them to read, write and spell. To help me in my task, I requested the names of the schools these children had previously attended and made an appointment to see each headmistress, who introduced me to the child's previous form teacher. They were very willing to help and whilst we chatted and they asked me what materials I would need, I had a quick look round to see what the children were using. I said I would need a supply of pencils, rubbers, copy books, reading books, sets of coloured wooden shapes, which they had to fit correctly into a tray. I also asked for an apron, modelling clay and a supply of paints and large brushes. I was determined to teach the older children how to write and spell well and to learn all their tables and weights and measures according to the capacity of the child. I am afraid

CHAPTER 6

I had a lot to learn myself.

The first child I went to teach was at an address in Ellesmere Port. The outside of the house was very neglected. Masses of matted grey grass grew in what had been a front garden. Everywhere there were dirty milk bottles and a large dilapidated springless couch lay on its side by a rotten wooden fence. I rang the bell. It was answered by a slatternly young woman in dirty clothes. I told her I was the home tutor and she asked me in and opened a door into the front room. It was entirely empty. There was no furniture and a large carpet, black with damp, lay on the floor. I turned to her and said, "*I must have some heating and a table and two chairs*". Then my first pupil walked in.

He was about seven years old and a mongol, but he gave me a cheery grin. The mother brought in a stove and a table and two chairs. I think Peter had never had such undivided attention before and he thrived on it. He was a cheery little boy and applied himself to learning. About 11 o'clock I was brought a cup of coffee in a chipped mug.

As the weeks progressed (I went there for two hours each week) the mother greeted me at the door looking cleaner and fresher and brought me tea in a china cup. Peter was always waiting at the door for my arrival and was so excited he had his arms held above his head, wriggling and smiling his obvious pleasure. I became quite fond of him.

Mary also lived in Ellesmere Port and her skin was like alabaster with blue veins clearly visible. She was also aged 7 but was very thin and fragile looking. I felt if I just touched her she would fall to pieces like the falling petals of a rose. I taught her in her little bedroom which was cheerful and sunny and I paced the lessons very quietly so as not to tire her. We talked a lot and she loved me to read any of the Beatrice Potter books, sitting close to me with her little head pressed against my shoulder. Like all my sick children she never whined or complained. It was as if she just took her condition for granted, which she probably did, having been like this since birth.

After about 6 months I arrived at her house one morning to see the front door wide open. Her mother came running out dreadfully distressed and saying, "*I can't go on like this any more, Mary has had three heart attacks in the night*". She ran on down the road to the phone box while I sat on the bottom step of the stairs gathering Mary in my arms on my lap. A few minutes later her mother returned saying the ambulance was on its way and she would pack her night clothes etc. She told me the specialist had been hoping Mary would have grown a little stronger before they had to perform hole-in-the-heart surgery. I hugged her close till we heard the shrill sound of the approaching ambulance, when she walked off holding her mother's hand and saying goodbye to me quite cheerfully.

The operation was performed a few days later at Alder Hey Hospital and she made a successful recovery, returning home some weeks later with her skin now a healthy pink. After a period of convalescence we returned to her lessons; she was eager to learn now and to be with her school friends. After some months I was able to report that Mary was up to standard and was ready to re-enter her local school.

Simon was a very different kettle of fish. I knew nothing about his medical condition. Aged about 11, he was tall, thin and constantly on the move and his head appeared to be too big for his body. He had difficulty keeping his hands still so I kept him writing as much as possible. The very first morning, after talking about what he did at school, he quite suddenly leapt up from the table and started to run round the room at speed. I called him back pretty severely and told him to sit down again. He didn't respond but after about three minutes he turned round quietly and came and sat down by me. I realised after a time that these attacks were quite uncontrollable so in future I didn't call him but waited for him to return and sit down.

His memory, such as it was, was quite unpredictable. When he was aged about 8 he had fallen into the canal near his home in Ellesmere Port and had been rescued by a boy of 15 who was passing. He remembered the whole incident vividly and told me the name of his rescuer, but he was quite incapable of remembering his sums or tables. He enjoyed reading, but it was only spasmodic as his concentration would lapse. It became quite obvious early on that Simon could never be taught in school. His behaviour, over which he had no control, was too disruptive. I discovered he was suffering from hydrocephalus, or water on the brain.

Well, I was here to teach him for two hours a week for a year and at least it took the pressure off his distracted mother. He had a kind of magpie intellect, following precisely certain tasks I set him to do one day and refusing to co-operate the next. So it was difficult to make any progress. I knew I had a calming effect on him and that the hours I spent with him had stimulated what little intelligence he had.

One day, when morning lessons had finished, his mother opened the door which went directly into the kitchen on whose table she had laid lunch for them both. Simon ran to it and before anyone could stop him swept all the dishes onto the floor. With his demented mother screaming he ran to me throwing his arms around me and burying his face on my chest. *"He doesn't know what he is doing"* I placated *"He can't help it"*. I helped her to pick the pieces up and insisted she sat down while I made a cup of tea. She sat there in her apron sobbing, he was her only child.

Josephine was as bright as a button. She was too fat for her age and was in the Ellesmere Port Cottage Hospital suffering from some form of kidney trouble. The hospital authorities had the bright idea of putting us in a room where a lot of very young children, in cots, were awaiting tonsil operations. Abandoned by their parents, the poor little frightened mites were standing up hanging onto the sides of their cots bawling their heads off. I walked in, quite obviously not a nurse, wearing my outdoor clothes and holding Josephine's hand *"Hello,"* I said, smiling at the children whilst moving two chairs round a table in the centre of the room. Almost immediately the crying stopped; here was something to watch.

We always did maths for the first half hour, starting with the 12 times table and weights and measures. Josephine loved geography, drawing and colouring the maps, which all the children enjoyed. Fortunately, I only taught her for six months as she had recovered so much in hospital she was allowed back to school.

The saddest case I ever took on was teaching a boy of 12 who was dying of leukaemia. I did not at first realise the seriousness of the illness. Although he looked a bit frail, I taught him all the usual subjects as he particularly wanted to sit the entrance exam to the King's School, Chester. The boy lived in a lovely house in the country with a beautiful garden. After I had been going there for about two months, his mother took me round the garden and it was there that she said she knew I was coaching him for his entrance exam but did I realise the seriousness of his illness. *"Yes"*, I said, *"but I must never let him know that and I will do everything I can to encourage and boost his morale"*. It wasn't easy and many a morning after a few lessons, I realised he wasn't well enough to carry on, so we sat on a couch and I put my arms around him and read to him.

One morning he had just come in with his mother who had a handful of pills, when he turned and ran out of the room looking distressed. His mother said, *"I am afraid he is going to be sick, he has to take so many pills a day that he has got to the stage that he vomits at the sight of them."* *"Let me have them every morning"*, I said, *"I will try to make a game of taking them"*. So that is what I did. I buried them in his favourite sweets and when he was least expecting it I popped one in his mouth. We never talked about them and if he had a bad headache I put them in a little cup pressed into marshmallows. He held the cup in his hand and I read to him or we sat together quietly.

He wanted so much to feel better and be able to go. back to school. He was intelligent and worked hard at his lessons on his good days. When he heard that he had passed his entrance exam to the King's School he was elated, but it was a bitter sweet pill for me and his parents. Gradually, he began to deteriorate and some lessons had to be abandoned, but I always popped in to see him and his parents until he was admitted to the Royal Infirmary. His mother rang me one day and begged me to come and see him as he was asking for me, so I went every day for a few hours to give his parents a rest from their agonising vigil.

The slow deterioration of the little body was pathetic to watch. He sort of melted away, bleeding from mouth, ears and eyes, he never cried but his pleading eyes were haunting. He was tended by a young, kind and sympathetic doctor who came in constantly to move him and wipe his face and try to make him more comfortable. His death was a merciful release but I felt as if I had lost a little pal, too. I had been with him for nearly a year and watched his brave battle against suffering.

The three children I taught at Ellesmere Port I found very exhausting. It was exacerbated by my own worries at this time and the depressing atmosphere of their surroundings. I longed to get away from the chipped concrete roads, derelict gardens choked with neglected grass and the abandoned milk bottles and paper that littered the gutters of that particular backwater of an otherwise much modernised, attractive town. If only I could find a way to lift the depression which was beginning to engulf me.

The direct route from my house in Hoole to Ellesmere Port was along the main road. Looking at a local map I discovered that I could cut across country on a back lane through Craughton, which consisted of a few farms and the hall, continue across the canal bridge below the zoo and rejoin the main road to Hoole.

Leaving Ellesmere Port the following day, I soon found the lane, which left the main road by a cottage, now connected to a small village and shop. The green of the grass and the peace and tranquillity of this lane worked like magic on my frayed nerves. It was springtime, and the hawthorn hedges were in flower. On the wide grass verges of the lane, cow parsley was beginning to burst into a foam of blossom. Old oak trees in the hedge threw their shadows across the grass and through the field gates I could see cows and rabbits in the fields on each side. As I hardly ever met anyone else in the lane I drove slowly and sometimes stopped the car and just looked and looked. It must be about four miles across country from one main road to the other and I enjoyed every minute of it.

Each week I called at a farm for eggs and whilst watching the free range hens foraging in the grass I spotted a stone trough and asked if I could buy it. *"That is the only one I have left"*, she confessed, *"we used them for feeding the calves, but the hens drink from it now. We threw them all in the pond at the back of the farm. I expect they are still there"*, she mused. Continuing down the lane, I passed the old sandstone wall of Craughton Hall at the foot of which borage nestled in abundance showing its bright forget-me-not blue flowers.

A little further on, where the lane narrows, a tiny pair of very damp-looking brick cottages huddled together like old friends on the top of the bank. There was a chimney at each end, two windows for each cottage, one above the other, and a steep flight of steps to the lane. I passed the cottages every day and wondered how they managed, so far away were they from water and food. Well, in the end they just fell down and were engulfed in brushwood, even the steps disappeared in long grass in no time at all. It was just as if no-one had ever lived there.

At the bottom of the lane I crossed the canal bridge, often stopping on the top to see if the flag iris were in flower or if there were any coots about. The steep bank up to the zoo was known as Butter Hill, because farm produce was left here for the beleaguered citizens of the City of Chester during the plague in 1704.

Five days a week, all through the year, I drove along that lane, stopping sometimes to watch a stoat cross the path, or in spring a hedge sparrow dive into the hawthorn hedge with a beak full of twigs for its nest. Every day there was something new to see as the wide grass verges were starched with Queen Anne's lace, then campion and the harsh gold of dandelions and ragwort beloved of the cinnabar moth. Willow herb and creamy meadowsweet grew in the ditches on each side.

As the leaves fell from the trees and scuttled across the road, the crimson of blackberries leaves began to show in the hedges which earlier had been festooned in places with the white horns of convolvulus. In winter the lane was often a sheet of ice. Fortunately, as there was little room to pass with deep ditches on each side, I hardly ever met another car. Whatever the time of the year, I knew, by the time I got to work, however demanding the day was going to be, I had so much to look forward to on my way home. There was also the satisfaction of knowing that I could help the children and give a few hours respite to a harassed parent.

Although I think I have never worked so hard as I did with these children who were in need of special tuition, I also benefited from the warmth and affection with which they greeted me. Deprived of health and often in pain, they never complained and I learnt a lot from their stoicism. That they came to depend on me, I accepted gratefully.

CHAPTER 7.

I had at last persuaded John to go and see his doctor. He came back saying, *"Robin says there is nothing wrong with me, I am just malingering"*.

"But that is an appalling thing to say to anyone," I said angrily, *"Did he give you a thorough examination?"*

"Yes", he said again, *"he could find nothing wrong with me"*.

"What are we going to do?" I groaned because whatever the doctor said, I did not think John looked really well.

Though he had a good appetite he was thin and gaunt. It was very hard to put into words why I was worried about his health but, being close to him, I knew things were not as they should be. I also knew it was not like John to be deliberately lazy. He could be his old charming self when we were with friends but when we were at home he was often withdrawn and seemed unable to concentrate. It was unheard of in those days to query a doctor's decision; they were like Gods, and, as he had said, *"There was nothing wrong with him"*, we could hardly request an appointment with a specialist, which we could not have afforded anyway, so I did the next best thing and made an appointment to see the doctor myself.

"John is not a malingerer" I said, *"I feel in some way the blood is not getting to his brain - he seems to be*

mentally lethargic."

"*Well*", said "Robin, "*there is nothing wrong with him. I have tested him thoroughly and he does not complain of feeling ill. I am afraid it is just John*".

"*Could he not be referred to a specialist?*" I enquired.

"*To what specialist?*", Robin replied irritably. "*It would only be wasting his time*".

Martin was now at Sedbergh. At least John was contributing something, selling insurance and with my salary as a home tutor, an income from a paying guest and whatever I could earn cleaning paintings and writing articles, we could manage. We reckoned that Martin would be due to leave Sedbergh by the time we wanted to send Vicki to boarding school, as there was a four year gap in their ages owing to our separation during the war.

As long as I could keep well, I felt we could manage, but worry was undermining me all the time and I had to fight it. Besides my morning work, I had shopping to do and meals to prepare each day for four of us and the usual chores of cleaning, ironing and generally running the house.

We had no Hoover when we were first married, so carpets had to be swept with a pan and brush. The space between the carpet and the wall, called 'the surround', had to be constantly dusted and repainted. We had no washing machine, fridge or dishwasher, but I do not think I ever felt the lack of them because we had never had them at home.

I took great pleasure in making the house as pretty and attractive as I could, always lots of flowers picked from the wild or from our garden. Excepting for my concern about John's health, we were very happy and had lots of friends with whom we played tennis and went hunting with the Royal Rock Beagles every Saturday in winter, the children coming with us from a very early age.

Joni now lived with Mum and Dad, but as both the men were out all day in Liverpool, I tried to visit Mum at Oxton about once a month. I kept up my writing and was encouraged by the Editor of the Wirral Journal, Kenneth Burnley. I also started to enter my watercolours in local exhibitions and selling them, which was very satisfying!

At the weekends in summer, John, Vicki and I visited some of the local boarding schools but had not come to any decision; not only were the fees above our means, but we did not feel that they would suit Vicki. We wanted a more homely atmosphere with a complement of about a hundred pupils and preferably situated in the country.

For many years Dad had been a member of a fishing club on the Elwy at Llangernyw in North Wales. It is a lovely little village surrounded by unspoilt country and when we stayed there as children, my parents took over all the bedrooms in the village inn. Dad and my brother, who was also a very keen fisherman, were staying at Llangernyw for a week's fishing and John and I were invited to fish with them at the weekend.

Sitting on the bank of the river one-day, I noticed four young girls hanging over the bridge looking into the water. They were wearing a very attractive grey uniform with a touch of turquoise at the neck of a jumper. Wondering where they came from I went up onto the bridge and spoke to them. *"We are from Hafodunos Hall, a boarding school up the valley behind Llangernyw,"* they smilingly replied. When I returned to the river I told John and we decided to make an appointment to visit the school.

Situated in glorious unspoilt country, Hafodunos Hall is reached up a long winding drive. Built by the Mackeson Sandbach family, the large handsome turreted Victorian building stands on a terrace with steps down to lower gardens and a deep valley, on the far side of which is a walled garden. Inside the columned entrance a beautiful tiled floor leads one to rooms whose long windows look out across the countryside.

The Mackeson Sandbach family had collected flowering trees from all over the world and the gardens were famous for the wild flowers in spring and the massed azaleas in every shade of peach, orange and yellow which grew below the terraces. Having been shown all over the school, we knew at once, that Vicki would be happy here in a few years' time.

With my brother and sisters I had roamed the fields and woods round Llangernyw and went with our parents to the village church which the school now attended on Sundays. In the churchyard stands the most ancient yew in the British Isles. In spring we had walked through the lychgate on Sundays on a path bordered by grass varnished gold with celandines and clumps of primroses. I knew Vicki would enjoy that.

Every experience we have in life, if we are receptive enough, can have a bearing on our future. Little did we know then that she was to become a Master of Horticulture and Landscape Architect.

In early summer Dad was taken ill with cancer of the throat. He fought it as long as he could but, eventually, he was admitted to Ruthin Castle, then a nursing home, and

*John and Vicki on the bridge over the River Elwy at
Llangernyw, close to Hafodunos Hall School.*

given a ground floor room looking onto the garden, but he
was very unhappy and longed to come home.

This was arranged, eventually, with a day and night
nurse in attendance. He dressed fully every day and sat in
the garden by the tennis court and the long rose bed,
reading. I went over frequently to sit with him and Mother

and I took it in turns to be with him. The family doctor called every evening at about six o'clock partaking of a sherry and chatting for an hour. My father died peacefully on 9th August 1948, aged 74.

Mother had now to be moved from her bedroom upstairs as her knees were so crippled with arthritis that she could no longer negotiate the steep flight of stairs. We moved her bedroom into the sitting room and she and Joni had their meals in the dining room where there was always a fire in winter and two comfortable fireside chairs.

Neither of them wanted to leave the old family home where we had all been so happy as children, and with so many memories, but now most of the eight bedrooms were closed up. Dad's study was still in use and was a lovely room to sit in looking onto the garden. All my sisters were married and had left home, but Amy, the housemaid, had stayed on to cook and look after Mother.

One morning the phone rang and a gentleman's voice enquired, "*I am the editor of Deesider, a local illustrated magazine, could I speak to Mrs Rocke?*"

"*Speaking*", I said somewhat puzzled.

"*I have had your name recommended to me and I wonder if you would care to write a monthly article on antiques for The Deesider*".

I was absolutely flabbergasted. Although I knew an antique when I saw one, I was by no means knowledgeable about such a vast subject, which covered furniture, pictures, silver and porcelain.

I thanked him and said I would like to think about it over the weekend and I put the phone down in a daze. It was too good an offer to turn down and someone else would do it if I didn't. Ever since I saw an old railway tankard on a shelf in a Welsh farmhouse and persuaded my father to buy it, I have been fascinated by old things.

Though the best reason for buying an antique is because you like it, your pleasure can be increased enormously by finding out as much as you can about it. We were living in a wonderful period for the collector of modest means. I think more people than ever were enjoying a little flutter at house sales and antique shops and acquiring some piece that would give them endless pleasure.

I decided over the weekend that my article would have to appeal to the average collector, the man or woman who, like myself, loved to poke round junk shops as well as the more expensive antique shops.

In my job as home tutor I came across many such shops in the Rock Ferry area of Birkenhead. Further afield, I found the Wirral Peninsula well stocked with bric-a-brac shops in many a side street. The shop-keepers were friendly and quite happy to let you poke around to your heart's content and, because the majority do not specialise in any particular field, it is a comforting fact that many of the dealers themselves know little or nothing at all about their wares.

Rich merchants and the cotton and shipping magnates had built large houses away from the docks, first along the riverside at Rock Ferry and then spread into the outlying villages of Bebington, Upton, Bidston and Oxton. From time to time the contents of these houses came on the market in house sales, of which there were usually two or three a week advertised in the local press. The dealers were able to buy quantities of articles, which were then considered to be old fashioned, very reasonably.

I decided to call my article "Antiques Down Your Way". This gave me an almost limitless field each month to write about bric-a-brac and antique shops situated in different parts of Wirral and Cheshire. I would enjoy interviewing the owners of the shops - I had had plenty of experience writing for Cheshire Life - and they in turn would be pleased to get a write-up in a well known magazine. What was more, I would expect to get a correct description and valuation of their wares.

I once hesitated and did not buy a Chester hall-marked silver rose bowl for £20, a large sum for me to pay in 1950. I decided later to return to the shop but, of course, it had been sold. Decisions often have to be made quickly because one rarely gets another chance. "If you feel a piece is right, buy it", I would advise my readers. It will always be worth the money you have spent on it.

When I told the editor on Monday of my decision and the title of my article, he was delighted and promised to provide me with a photographer.

CHAPTER 8

The decision to write for The Deesider turned out to be of far greater benefit than I could possibly have envisaged. It opened up a whole new and exciting experience and I was hooked for life.

As I was teaching a child near Neston in Wirral I decided I would call on the antique shops there, for my first article, and then pop down to Parkgate, the ancient fishing village on the Dee, to buy some shrimps for supper. Driving down the main Neston to Parkgate road I noticed that an antique fair was in progress in a Church hall on the left hand side of the road. Parking the car I went in, paying my 3d entrance fee! There were about twenty stalls selling an enormous variety of wares from brass and copper, linen, porcelain, glass, buttons, to figurines and books, which stall was run by an old Etonian! A vicar's wife had another stall and the whole atmosphere was open and friendly.

I introduced myself to Mrs Lea Moulden, who was running the fair, and asked her if she would like me to give her fair a write-up in Deesider. She was delighted and asked me if I would care to take a stall next Saturday in return.

I jumped at the idea, though at that time I had nothing to sell. However, writing for Deesider and visiting antique and bric-a-brac shops for material for my articles, I quickly realised the opportunity I would have to pick up enough pieces to stock a stall the size of a pasting table which was the area allotted. When I got home I rang my friend Jo, who lives in Burton village and was a keen and knowledgeable collector, to see if she would like to join me for my first stall. She agreed and promised to bring something to sell.

I walked round the fair and looked at the goods for sale and the prices asked. I suppose I had an advantage in that I had been interested enough to read the copiously illustrated reference books on collecting china from my father's library when I was quite young.

Like Dad, I had developed an eye for quality. I knew instinctively what pieces were genuine and valuable and I had a strong gut feeling that many of the pieces of porcelain for sale on the stalls were undervalued. There was a glut on the market of Staffordshire, Minton, Crown Derby and Wedgwood, comprising part dinner and tea services and dressing table sets purchased in Victorian house sales. At that time I could buy a green Wedgwood leaf plate for about one shilling. I decided, as I had little money to spend, that I would only buy pieces that I liked and which, if possible, were marked with the name of the manufacturer. There was an abundance of pretty plates, dishes and jugs which came from tea sets, also vegetable dishes, gravy boats and soup tureens, some without lids, which had been part of a dinner service and could be picked up for shillings and made attractive containers for flower arranging. Jo and I did very well with our first stall, almost selling out. We copied the more experienced stall holders the following week, by displaying goods on benches in front and with extra tables at the side.

It was great fun writing for Deesider. I met a lot of antique dealers who gave me useful information, helping me to identify pieces, but I never got the hang of hard and soft porcelain! Sadly, the job lasted only a year as the Editor was unable to continue its publication. He found there was not enough demand in the county for two similar publications. Cheshire Life, having been on sale for some years, had a monopoly of the market - but the contacts made and the knowledge I gained were invaluable.

During my visits to junk shops I was asked if I had heard of the Sunday Antique Market at Runcorn New Town. I was told it was worth a visit.

This antique market was held in a large open area in the middle of the new shopping complex, the shops, of course, all being closed on Sundays. It opened at 8 o'clock. I decided to go early on Sunday morning and go in with the dealers. There were a lot of stalls being set up, some by slightly suspect-looking people. I soon got the impression that some of the goods were stolen, but as far as I was concerned, it was the chance of a lifetime! Everything had to be examined with the greatest care. Most of the china was unwashed so it was not easy to see cracks. Copper and brass pieces were unpolished and often black. If I looked carefully I found pewter mugs and sometimes silver pieces that were so dirty the stall holder had not even bothered to find the assay marks. Little figurines were sold for a song because they needed a slight repair and there were many damaged oil paintings and engravings in shoddy frames needing attention. The stall holders were a cheerful, ignorant and happy crowd, delighted to sell anything. As for me, I bought and bought and bought.

Amongst the boxes of cutlery I often found a piece of silver that had been overlooked. There were also many small pieces of furniture, bookcases, stools, small tables, wooden cutlery boxes with handles and an assortment of wooden boxes of all sorts such as tea caddies and jewellery boxes. Often the goods were slightly damaged so were sold very cheaply. John was a great help with any woodwork that needed repair. Staffordshire ware could be bought very cheaply especially the pastille burners and groups of figurines supporting a spill holder. As the top of the spill holder was often snapped off they could be bought for a few shillings but became very collectable twenty years later.

To a great extent one had to know the market. If I had had unlimited cash there was no doubt that I could have bought things that I knew then would not sell, but put away for years, would be fashionable again. For instance, I saw quantities of white embroidered and lace-edged tablecloths, grubby and piled in heaps selling at about 2/6 each. The leisurely grace of the Victorian afternoon tea parties had died with the war. Not having any need for them, as I had inherited some of my Mother's, I did not buy any but later wished that I had. The wheel goes full circle and many objects that were once looked upon as old-fashioned are now much in demand. It is not very easy to be always one jump ahead and I couldn't afford to take risks. I was in the business to improve my bank balance.

It was very exciting unwrapping all my purchases when I got home. If I was lucky I even picked up a Spode plate for a few shillings. Carefully washed and polished I often got ten times more than I had paid for an article. If I thought a piece was really valuable I took it to a friend I had met when writing for Deesider, who ran a lovely antique shop in the country, and whom I could trust to pay me a good price. I think I had the most fun with the paintings which I was able to clean and re-varnish, washing the incredibly dirty glass and repairing and restoring the frames where possible. I also learnt from a book how to clean dirty and fox-marked prints and engravings.

On the Saturday stall at Neston I usually took about £100 or more. I banked nearly all the money every week. I never found the work of restoration tiring. It was always rewarding and exciting, for in this I saw my children's future and something I could give them for life and which John and I had been privileged to experience. I went to Runcorn every Sunday morning for years, becoming completely absorbed and always finding it well worth while. I suppose I became like a smoker or an alcoholic, unable to give it up though I never stayed more than a couple of hours, returning about 11.30 to get Sunday lunch ready. If Martin was home for half-term and it was a lovely summer afternoon we went into Wales for a walk and a picnic supper.

I had been worried about my brother for some time as he was inclined to drink too much; I suppose it's the prerogative of most of the sailing fraternity. I was not prepared, however, for the news from Mike Webster, his great friend and member of his crew, who rang me about 4 o'clock one summer evening to tell me Joni had been taken ill on board Dolphin during a race. They had to return to Rock Ferry and call an ambulance. He was taken to the Wallasey Cottage Hospital. He thought he had had an attack of food poisoning. I immediately rang the hospital and spoke to the Ward Sister. "*Are you a relative?*" she enquired and on being told that I was his sister, she advised me to come as soon as possible. It was Saturday afternoon so I told John what had happened and said that he would have to get supper ready for Vicki and the paying guest and that I was going over immediately to the hospital.

When I arrived I was taken at once to the side ward

where Joni, still dressed in his sailing gear, was lying on a stretcher with his eyes closed. I took hold of his hand; it was stone cold. *"Joni"*, I said, *"it's Liz"* (my family pet name). He opened his eye a bit but did not move. After some time a nurse came in. I went out with her into the corridor. *"What's happened?"* I asked. *"His hand is like ice, can't you put a blanket over him?"*

She took me to the Sister's room. *"Your brother,"* she said, *"has had a very serious heart attack, we cannot move him at present"*. *"What are his chances?"* I blurted out. *"We cannot tell, the next 24 hours are critical"*. Immediately I thought of Mother - what was I going to tell her?

As there was nothing more I could do, I left my telephone number with the hospital and drove to Bidston Road. Mum was surprised to see me and, not wanting to alarm here too much, I said Joni had had a bad bilious attack and Mike had taken him to hospital where they would be keeping him in for observation and that I would pop over and see her again tomorrow. Thankfully, Amy was there to get her meal so she was not alone, but the implications were extremely worrying.

Joni's life hung in the balance for three days. When he was out of immediate danger he was placed in a ward. Now I could tell Mum the truth. She took it very well and, as I had been allowed to see him that day, I could tell her that he was cheerful but not allowed to lift a finger. After a month he began to improve but Sister said he would be there for some months more.

On my last visit to Mum, Amy told me she wished to retire. I spoke to Mother about Amy and suggested we advertised for a companion help, at least till Joni was well enough to come home. I was relieved that Mother agreed and we put an advertisement in the Birkenhead News.

We had four replies and I arranged interviews at Mother's house when I could be there. Amy promised not to leave till we had Mother fixed up. Out of the four applicants Mother quickly made her choice. She was a charming capable widow called Mrs Peters aged about 60, kindly and well spoken. She turned out to be an absolute treasure, often bringing special little meals she had prepared at her home a few miles away. It was a great weight off my mind.

I visited Joni when I could and found him sitting up at last and giving me a cheeky grin. He pulled up the sheet to reveal a half bottle of whisky by his feet. *"Joni"* I said in alarm, *"are you allowed it?"* Although, as I asked him, I realised the nurses must have known. *"Sure,"* he said, *"we are allowed a wee nip from time to time,"* reverting to his Irish brogue. I knew Joni was on the mend then.

He was in hospital for another two months and went to the home of one of his crew mates to convalesce. His doctor had told him that he should think about moving into a flat as he felt it was too much of a strain for him looking after Mother. Poor Joni, he knew that moving away would be a severe blow to Mother but the constant frustration of his partial immobility and Mother's deafness had taken its toll. He had turned to whisky for consolation. I never felt Joni was the marrying sort and he felt no girl would want him with his gammy leg. Mother would miss him dreadfully but she was very understanding and really wanted him to have his own home.

Joni was Commodore of the West Cheshire Sailing Club in 1961 and Dolphin was moved into the yard. He wanted to live near the sea and looked for a flat in the New Brighton/Wallasey area as some of his crew lived locally. A first floor flat was advertised in North Drive in an area of large, handsome Victorian houses overlooking the sea and with steeply sloping long gardens which extended to the newly constructed promenade. By sheer chance the owner of the house, who lived on the ground floor with her son, had known my father many years ago so she was delighted to let the flat to Joni.

A long flight of steps up the front of the house gave access to the flat. The sitting room on the front had a window with a panoramic view across the Mersey. Another window facing west looked up the Welsh coast. You could see the Great Orme on a clear day. There was a bedroom and kitchen on this floor. The rent also included the whole of the top floor where there was a bathroom and a large room which Joni used as a workroom and the two other bedrooms were used for a guest and as a sail locker.

To furnish the flat, Mother arranged for all his bedroom furniture to be sent over and told Joni he could take anything he liked from Dad's study. She also gave him the 18th century sideboard from the dining room and a large dining room table and six leather chairs which had come from 'Ellesmere'. Mother let him chose which of the paintings he would like to take. He chose only four, knowing we four girls should have our share one day. The heavy velvet curtains from Dad's study he used for his bedroom. Well, that was Joni sorted out.

Mother now realised that she would have to sell the old house and said she would like to come and live with me. I had been aware of this possibility for some time but, although John and I were happy to have Mum living with us, it meant a lot of extra work for me and, frankly, I just didn't know how I was going to be able to cope. I was fully stretched as it was. *"Johnnie,"* I said, *"if Mum comes to live with us we will have to sell Kilmorey, (our house in Hoole), as Mum will need a downstairs bedroom. It will mean looking for a house with three reception rooms. Mum will have to help us financially, which I am sure she will."*

I felt as if I were on a kind of roller coaster and I wanted to get off. For one thing I knew I would have to give up my Home Tutor job and with it a salary which was not only financially helpful but reliable too. Jo and I were both doing well at Neston and now we had a stall each. I saw no reason why I should not continue my trips to Runcorn on Sunday morning. It was exciting and remunerative and I could hardly wait to see what was for sale each week. I always returned with a boot full of purchases, nearly all of which would need repair or cleaning, but the results were so satisfying that I never begrudged the time it took.

Mother was anxious to put her house on the market as soon as possible, not wanting to spend another winter there. I begged her to wait until I had had time to look for a suitable property for us all and to put our own house up for sale. We would then have a better idea of what sort of property we could afford between us. We wanted to stay in Chester.

We advertised our house for sale with a well known Chester estate office, asking double what we had paid for it as sitting tenants. We felt we had a lot to offer as we were within easy walking distance of the shops and station but secluded in a quiet road overlooking gardens. In a panic I realised I must notify the estate agents of the kind of property we were seeking. We required a minimum of three reception rooms and at least four bedrooms.

There is something about estate agents that I will never understand. It is as though they go out of their way to send details of properties which have nothing to do with the specific description of the house we were looking for. They have to be cajoled. I rang the estate agents urging them, as politely as possible, to refer to the details in my letter. Most afternoons now I spend tidying up the bedrooms and cleaning the bathroom of our house in the hope that I would soon be showing potential buyers around.

One day in November one of the estate agents rang me to say a house had just come on to their books which he thought might interest me and that he would meet me there with the key that afternoon if I was agreeable. The house looked very promising from the outside, set in extensive gardens and with a large detached stable block which I thought we could sell. However, when we went inside I saw there were only two reception rooms; we would have to build on.

As we returned to the hall feeling disconsolate, the agent said, *"I don't know whether you know but the house on the other side of the road, called Harlow, is up for sale privately. The owner is in a home and the married children, realising that it is unlikely that their Mother will be able to return, had been forced reluctantly to sell the family home which has only been lived in occasionally for the last 15 years"*. It was now in need of much restoration. He said he could get a key and meet us there the following day.

CHAPTER 9

After the agent had left John and I looked at one another and decided we would cross the road and have a look round the outside of the house as it was empty. As we were walking up the drive I suddenly stopped dead. *"John,"* I said in a mixture of amazement and excitement, *"this is the house we saw as children from the road outside where the trees were surrounded with white railings. We used to shout, 'there is the house with the trees with the corsets on'"*. I went back outside and the trees were there but the white railings had gone, no doubt, in the war effort. We stood in the drive looking at the front of the house. Everything we saw pleased us. It was two storied and built of mellow brick.

As the children had heard my story about the house we decided to get the key at the weekend and all go in together. It was a cold November day but we hardly noticed. A short flight of steps led to an oak door set in a sandstone surround. Inside a square porch with side windows and a red tiled floor led to a glass-topped door which opened into the main hall. Large windows lit the hall which continued down the west side of the house to a big sitting room which originally had been two rooms. It had a pretty bay window on the front of the house and two more on the side wall.

All the windows in the house had leaded lights, many of which were broken. Grey faded paper hung off the walls and the large heating pipes had many cracks in them through which water had escaped some years before. Sticks and moss which had come down the sitting room chimney

75

lay halfway across the floor and part of the mahogany mantelpiece was rotten, but it was a beautifully proportioned room and we all loved it right away.

Next to this room was a study or smoking room. The fireplace surround was a pale carved oak and reached from floor to ceiling. In the west wall, looking onto the fields, was a lovely window with stone transoms and a window seat. Another window looked down the garden. Next door was a cloakroom. This would be an ideal room for Mother.

The floor of the hall and corridors was covered with parquet flooring which, because it appeared to have been covered with a wall to wall carpet, was a lifeless grey colour. On the right hand side of the front door was a large square dining room with a floor to ceiling window at the front of the house. Blue and white Dutch tiles surrounded the fireplace.

We went down the corridor to the kitchen quarters. The first room on the left had been the butler's pantry. The floor had collapsed revealing 6 feet of water in the cellar below. All the mahogany shelves and fittings had been torn from the walls and lay on the floor of the passageway. A door opposite led to the kitchen and scullery. There was an old range here which had been torn from the chimney bay and lay on the floor. There were no wall fittings or cupboards. In the scullery an old porcelain sink stood beneath the window and steps led down to an outside lavatory and coal house, all very neglected and dirty.

A back staircase led up from the end of the corridor to what appeared to be a nursery wing as there was a little gate at the top of the stairs. There was no window on these stairs which made it a very gloomy area. There were eight bedrooms on the landing above, two lavatories and a separate bathroom. At the end of the kitchen corridor there was an entrance to the larder with a slate slab and an apple store. Another short corridor led to a two storey timber building at the rear of the house. It was lit by gas mantles and presumably had been added as servants' quarters.

Then we looked around the garden. An old greenhouse had most of the panes broken and there were two old sheds and some derelict hen-houses. A cinder track led past the stable yard to the fields at the back where the last owners kept their horses. There was a large lawn suitable for a tennis court and an orchard full of very old trees. Excepting for some rhododendrons in the shrubbery lining the road, most of the garden was a wilderness and covered with willowherb. We reckoned there was at least an acre and a half of land comprising all the garden at the front and rear of the house.

On the left side of the drive a large empty border stretched along the field fence ending in a magnificent beech tree. On the front lawn there were four ten foot long rose borders, now sadly neglected. Inside the fence there were tall beech, sycamore, holly and four fir trees screening the house from the road which still had the bands of grass along the verge as I remembered it 48 years before.

At the side of the house there was a stable yard, the entrance to which was guarded by a wall and square brick piers topped by stone balls. The stable had been built parallel to the house and was a substantial building with stabling for two horses, a tack room with fireplace and ample accommodation upstairs for a groom. An interesting feature in the stable yard was a large wheel with a handle on the outside wall of the coal shed. In front on the ground a large concrete slab covered the entrance to a very deep well, now devoid of water.

I wondered what quirk of fate had brought us to this

house. It was the sort of home both John and I had been used to living in as children and, had it not been in such a bad state of repair and therefore on the market at a very reasonable price, we could never have afforded such a property. That we had all fallen in love with it was evident but there was going to be a mammoth task ahead and what a challenge it would be to restore it.

We all returned home very excited and I rang Joni and asked him to come over and inspect it for dry rot. We had had experience of that in Bidston Road when four rooms had to have all the plaster removed when fungi, caused by leaking pipes, had been discovered in the cloakroom. The spores had spread like wild fire beneath the plaster from room to room. Joni had been in hospital at the time and on his return had gone into the cloakroom. To his horror he saw three large mushrooms on the mahogany surround of the basin and knew immediately what it was.

We all returned on Monday evening with Joni who went from room to room poking into floors, skirting boards and door surrounds with a penknife. Like us, he fell for the house and realised the study would make a perfect room for Mother. Between us we listed everything that would need to be done starting with essentials and priorities.

1. A pump would have to be fitted in the cellar.

2. All the central heating pipes had to be removed.

3. The floor to be replaced in the Butler's pantry.

4. The timber building at the back had to be removed as soon as possible as Joni was sure it had been a contributory factor to the dry rot.

5. All the plumbing, bathroom pipes etc needed

attention. The plumbers were to find two huge tanks under the roof. One was rusty and had no water in it and the other needed scaling and cleaning out.

6. The parquet floor would need sanding and sealing with a special hard drying varnish before any furniture could be delivered.

7. We decided to put a coke stove in the kitchen bay where the old range had been. This would heat the water and provide a warm and welcoming room. A sink and draining boards would need to be fitted under the window with cupboards below. A gas cooker would need to be installed. The scullery and larder could be attended to later.

8. All the chimneys had to be swept before a fire could be lit in the sitting room or gas fires installed in the other downstairs rooms. Gas was already laid on to all rooms.

9. Joni had found dry rot in the study window and in two treads on the back staircase which would need cutting out and replacing.

Replacing the broken panes, painting and papering, we would have to do ourselves as much as possible. The stable could wait. Fortunately, the house had been rewired and the roof was sound. We couldn't get away from the fact that we would need gallons and gallons of emulsion paint for the walls. Every single room, hall, passage way and staircase wall needed painting. We decided we would get a decorator in to paint all the ceilings white. We had counted the doors which needed repainting and there were twenty two. At the rate of two undercoats each side and one topcoat, we had one hundred and thirty two doors to paint!

The treads on each side of the stair carpet were painted white and had to be renewed, as did most of the windowsills. It was no exaggeration to say that there seemed to be miles of skirting board. Never had the poignant advice of my father been so apposite as when, seeing me struggling to come to terms with some problem, he had remarked, *"Don't think about it, just do it"*.

How on earth were we going to pay for all the work that needed to be done before we could even think of moving in? We simply hadn't got the money. Vicki was now at Hafodunos Hall and Martin had a year to go at Sedbergh. I knew that eventually I would have to give up my tutoring job when Mother came to live with us. Although I was glad to look after Mother the extra responsibility appalled me as she was more or less chair-ridden. John was becoming more and more of a responsibility and at times seemed almost childishly pathetic. He had no job now and because he was not registered disabled he was unable to apply for any benefit. Although I was almost at the end of my tether not knowing what was wrong with him and from time to time voicing my feeling of exasperation, he never tried to defend his behaviour and would behave a bit like a beaten dog, saying nothing. I couldn't bear it.

Again I begged him to go and see the doctor who decided to send him to a psychiatrist. When he came back I asked him how he had got on. *"Well"*, said John, *"he asked me if I was happy to which I replied, yes. Then he asked had I any worries and I replied, Not really"*. In other words it was a complete waste of time. There was nothing I could say. I loved him and never wanted to be parted from him. My responsibilities were so great that I think I just put my head in the sand, railing against his behaviour only made us both unhappy and resolved nothing.

He was not yet fifty and should have been in his

prime. He always looked what he was, a perfect country gentleman, very proud of his family. He frequently wore wool stockings to the knee and Harris Tweed breeches which suited his tall figure and long legs. He was comfy to be with. If the doctor said there was nothing wrong with him, perhaps he would rally in the end. I could only look forward to the future when I longed so much to live with him in a little country cottage.

We had asked Mother and Joni to come and stay with us for Christmas. On Christmas Eve with a house full the front door bell rang. It was a mother and daughter who wanted to see over Kilmorey, our house in Hoole, with intent to purchase. I apologised for the untidiness, and so did they for calling at such an inconvenient time, saying they did not need to go into every room but just make a quick assessment of the accommodation. I took them round, they implied approval and left.

We took Mother to see Harlow. She was delighted with the house and with the room we had decided would be hers. We also showed her all the work that needed to be done before we could even contemplate moving in.

Two days after Christmas I had a phone call from my estate agent informing me that a Mrs Venables, who had called on Christmas Eve, had offered the asking price. The money would be paid into the bank in four weeks on condition that we vacated the house on the same date. Now my hand was forced. I had no alternative but to buy Harlow as quickly as possible. I rang up Mum who was delighted and promised to pay for most of the essential repairs and to pay her share of the purchase price. I begged her not to be too hasty in selling her house as I would have an enormous amount to do before I was ready to move her too. Also, it was imperative that I kept up my monthly articles for Deesider and my weekly visits to Runcorn for my Saturday stall. I still had my paying guest who decided to move with us. I spoke to my solicitor who arranged for my purchase of Harlow to go through immediately. On being told that a down payment would be paid into their bank immediately the owners of the house kindly promised to let us have a key and start repairs immediately. The purchase price also covered the replacement of the floor in the butler's pantry.

Though I had signed the agreement with the solicitor for the purchase of Harlow, I did so with a sinking heart. Whatever was I letting myself in for? However, John, Martin and Vicki were so supportive and enthusiastic, promising to help as it was the Christmas holidays, that some of my fears were calmed.

We collected the key the following day. I had already rung a firm who supplied pumps and arranged for one to be fitted within a week. I had contacted a firm of plumbers and spoken to a well known coal merchant in Chester who came round to give us advice about fitting a coke stove in the kitchen. I had booked a removal firm to collect our furniture from Hoole.

By the time the four of us entered the house we were all feeling like explorers embarking on an expedition. It was a cold day but the sun was shining. We all went into the sitting room where streaks of sunlight fell across the floor. I decided to light a fire. "*Is it really ours, Mum?*" Vicki enquired hopefully, "*Yes, it is*", I replied, whereupon she began to tear great stripes of faded wallpaper off the sitting room walls with a joyous abandon. We all laughed and then started choking and coughing as smoke poured out from the chimney and lumps of sticks and grass fell onto the hearth. We realised there was probably fifteen years of starlings' nesting material packed down the chimney. In the end we had to have the chimney sweep three times before it was cleared properly.

I had taken a Thermos and some buns for tea. John, who was very good at wall papering, had started to measure up the large sitting room to see how many rolls we would need and Martin was counting how many pieces of glass he would need to replace those broken in the leaded lights, when the bell rang at the front door. I went along to see who it was and a man about John's age introduced himself rather shyly, saying he had put the house on the market and, as he was passing had plucked up courage to see who was going to live in his parents' old home.

I immediately asked him in, apologising for our old clothes and said, *"Come and meet my husband and the family"*. As he walked into the sitting room and saw John his face lit up with pleasure. *"John Rocke, have you bought our house?"* He had met John when he was in the cutlery business and he was delighted that we were coming to live there. We went into the study at the back of the house where there was the window seat and had some tea and talked about the house and what we intended to do, whilst Martin and Vicki ran upstairs to choose their bedrooms.

During the next few weeks I contacted a firm who sanded parquet flooring and impressed upon them the importance of leaving at least two days after the varnish had been applied, so that it would be quite dry, before the furniture van was due.

The plumbers arrived in the first week and were in the house for ten days. They were very co-operative and the first day kindly removed the old range and the fittings from the butler's pantry and the gas cooker into one of the sheds in the stable yard. I felt the first priority was to get the kitchen walls painted before the stove and gas cooker were delivered. Allan Morris, coal merchants, arranged for a suitable stove to be delivered when the plumbers were in the house. They also supplied us with a load of coal and coke which was conveniently stored in the shed provided at the foot of the stairs leading from the back kitchen door.

As we had decided to use Mother's old rose carpet for the sitting room we chose a soft old rose pink paper with a faint silvery stripe. That kept John happy for ages as he had eleven rolls to be pasted and hung. Martin continued repairing the leaded windows. I was given the name of a good joiner, an old man, but skilled. He cut out the rotten piece of mantelpiece and lowered the top shelf. Then he tackled the cills that had to be cut out and replaced in the study. We decided to leave the treads on the back staircase until later.

I persuaded a decorator to come just to paint the kitchen ceiling, promising him further work. As it was the school holidays I was excused from teaching for three weeks. This was a great help and after we had all been to the Boxing Day Meet of the Royal Rock Beagles and told our friends about the house, we were inundated with offers of help.

My great friend Doreen Bramble said she would come over every day from Guilden Sutton in Wirral and help me to paint the kitchen. We had met during the war years at the Western Command when she was a FANY and I was in the local service ATS. I nearly filled the car boot with gallons of emulsion, undercoat and gloss paint. I also bought a supply of brushes, turpentine and fine sand paper for rubbing down. The bottom three feet of the walls in the kitchen corridor were painted dark brown which we decided to get rid of. Whilst friends tackled these walls with emulsion and gloss paint, Doreen and I started on the kitchen. When we were in the middle of this a man arrived to fit the stove so we went into the corridor to help. Thank goodness the sweep had returned to clear the sitting room chimney.

We had collected planks which we rested on stools and also a garden seat and we all sat round the fire to eat the lunch which I had provided for the helpers. We had mugs of tomato soup, meat pies and Eccles cakes and buttered buns. Martin and his friend Tiggie had been painting his bedroom walls and Vicki had washed quite a few window sills and frames to her satisfaction, and ours too, because she realised some of them were not too bad and didn't need repainting at present. I had brought an electric kettle over to make tea and coffee for friends and workmen. On Sunday about six beaglers turned up. By then, thank goodness, the stove had been fitted and we had lots of hot water and the kitchen was warm. All morning there was the sound of doors being rubbed down and undercoats slapped on with much laughter. Jimmy McGuinness allotted to spend a day on the back staircase ripping off old linoleum and lifting hundreds of tacks.

I had been to Runcorn as usual very early, filling the boot with a mixture of china, glass, copper and brass articles all of which needed attention but would have to wait till I got home. We all sat round the sitting room fire again discussing the merits of the day's hunting the day before and eating hungrily. I had to get in the supplies sometime during the week, tins of Heinz tomato soup, meat pies, bread rolls, fruit and buns or fruit cake, coffee and beer. Friends sometimes brought contributions of cakes or cheese.

I was unable to find a firm to demolish the timber building, but that could wait. Friends came every Sunday and Doreen and I continued painting the kitchen and passage way. At last, a week before we were to move in, the kitchen sink and cupboards were fitted. We had painted the large window which looked onto the stable yard.

As soon as the plumbers had finished I arranged for my home help to come for a day to clean the bathroom and all the loos, of which there were five. Somehow, having people all over the house made it already feel like home. She brushed out all the downstairs rooms and cleaned all along the sitting room skirting board where the heating pipes had been removed. Joni had come over for a day and was painting the skirting boards in the sitting room so that John could finish the papering.

On the last week before the move I was getting anxious about the sanding of the parquet flooring. I rang the firm to remind them that the furniture would be coming in on Friday. Midday on Wednesday the firm arrived and that gave the varnish barely 36 hours to dry. When the sanding was finished and varnish applied the parquet looked glorious, a shining golden honey colour. In order not to walk on the hall those two days we went through the back door to the kitchen and through the study window to reach the sitting room. We had already had Martin's and Vicki's bedroom carpets re-laid but all the other carpeting would be coming from Mother's house.

On Friday John stayed at Kilmorey whilst I was at Harlow to instruct the men in which room to place the furniture, pictures etc. That evening I returned to Kilmorey to find to my horror that they had left a lot of things behind. On each side of the kitchen fireplace, the large cupboards from floor to ceiling had not even been opened. They were full of china. The iron Victorian garden seat had also been left. I rang the firm and arranged for them to collect on Saturday morning. They were not too pleased and I was thankful that the houses were only a mile apart.

CHAPTER 10

We moved house at the end of January on a fine cold day. Of the three bedrooms in the front of the house, John and I chose the large one with a wash basin and Vicki had the corresponding room on the other corner of the house. In between was a very quaint room, long and narrow with windows the whole length of one wall looking onto the drive. In the corner of the room was an ancient gas fire which we found very intriguing, as the top opened up to reveal a gas cooking ring. We decided to make this room into an upstairs sitting room, a sort of den, in which we would have the television. The large sitting room could be used for entertaining or in the summer when we could dispense with a fire. Mother's pink carpet would only cover two-thirds of the room but I found a firm who would dye my sitting room carpet to match. Fortunately all the curtain rails were there and, as our bedroom at Kilmorey had much bigger windows, we could get by with the curtains we had for the present.

It was good to be in but we were heartily sick of painting doors and called a truce. However, friends continued to come at the weekends. One enjoyable job they tackled was to clean all the brass taps which the plumbers had wanted to replace with modern ones but, knowing how much more efficient they would be compared with the modern equivalent, I refused to have them replaced. Also we found that all the brass door furniture and door knobs had been painted over with white paint so that had to be removed too, much to our satisfaction.

John and I more or less camped out in our bedroom. It was a very large room with a flowery wallpaper. At this stage we couldn't afford a carpet so we put down a few rugs on the bare boards. Mother's very big house was carpeted all through so there would be enough with ours to furnish the house. There was so much still to be done, though, before then. We had at last had the timber building removed and all the painted tongue and groove planks stacked in the stable.

One of the first things I wanted to get done was to have a window inserted on the back staircase wall to let light into the very dark corridor and nursery wing upstairs. I was thankful for the large china cupboard and shelves in the wall of the downstairs corridor as, at that time, we had no storage cupboards in the kitchen though there was an excellent larder. I asked the decorator who was painting the dining room and kitchen ceilings if he would paint the whole kitchen with two coats of white emulsion. Once that was done my home help scrubbed all the tiled kitchen and larder floors.

In order to make the bedrooms easier to decorate we decided to remove all the Victorian iron fireplaces except one which was pretty with a round top. We tried selling them to antique shops but had no luck. In the end we threw them down the empty well in the stable yard with dozens of Kilner jars from the tack room (I had lots of my own), and broken panes from the greenhouse. The well became a useful dumping ground for old broken garden tools we found in the sheds and rubbish from the coach house.

It didn't occur to us at this stage why the underside of the coach house roof was draped with loops of sheeting but with the coming of the spring the swallows arrived swooping in all day to build their nests in the rafters. The windscreen of the car was plastered with droppings in their flight to the roof. They also nested in the kitchen porch. House martins built their nests under the eaves on the garden side of the house and we loved the sound of their twittering. Having lived before in a town house with only a few sparrows, this wilderness of a garden with its fruit trees was a paradise for birds. We had nuthatches, flycatchers, and woodpeckers nesting in a tall fir tree. Bullfinches pecked the buds on the apple trees and chaffinches and blue tits darted about amongst the seed heads.

As the long border from the gate against the field fence was devoid of plants I went over to Mother's house, not yet on the market, and dug up lots of perennials. I brought them home in cardboard boxes and stored them under the open glass porch in front of the house. Although we had quite a frost that winter they survived and bit by bit I got them planted including plants brought from friends' gardens.

I think the land at the end of the orchard had been used for growing vegetables. There were no plants but the ground was hard ridged and in one corner was quite a deep pond full of tree branches and surrounded by old willows, many of whose branches lay scattered on the grass. I stepped carefully and suddenly a great surge of joy went through me - snowdrops. In a patch about a yard square they were pushing their way up through the grass. On my way back along the overgrown field hedge I watched a blackbird tossing the dead oak leaves aside. They were wet underneath and he thrust his bill deep into the ground for insects. Automatically, I too, kicked the loose leaves and uncovered bright green spurs of daffodils stretching about a yard wide the whole length of the hedge. That was all I needed, the weeds could wait.

We decided to cover the dining room walls with a rich

deep blue figured paper, picking up the colour of the Delph blue tiles and the Chinese blue and white dishes which were to be displayed on my dresser when they arrived from Mother's house. There was a lot of light in this room coming from the long windows on the front of the house and the two side windows. All the paintwork was white and I couldn't wait to see the Donegal carpet with its rich colours on the floor and the long velvet apricot coloured curtains.

One evening at dusk, Martin walked out of the back door intending to go down the steps to the garden to collect some firewood. He came back a few seconds later into the kitchen saying, *"There's a fox at the bottom of the steps in the garden and it looks very ill"*. We all went out to have a look. The poor animal stood shivering, its head hanging down. Martin went to the phone and rang the RSPCA but they were closed. From the police we got the name of a vet on call and rang him but he refused to attend as he said it was vermin and recommended that we approached it with the utmost care as it was no doubt poisoned.

We couldn't leave it there in the bitter cold so Martin managed to get a noose round its neck and gently walked it into the stable where we put a sack over its back and left some water. The following morning we opened the heavy door and were puzzled to find no sign of the fox. Some weeks later on opening the stable door Martin was assailed with a most awful stench. We then guessed what had happened, the fox had crawled behind the stacks of timber to die. As we had tried unsuccessfully to sell all the timber and as every piece had to be removed to find the body of the fox, we piled the lot onto the cinder horse track to the fields and set fire to them.

Work slowly progressed in the house and Vicki and

Martin, with friends, continued to decorate their bedrooms. It was a great relief to have the cellar dry, the pump worked to perfection, never allowing the water to come above a level in the sump. The floor above had been replaced. I was back to teaching in the mornings.

My antiques trade was a Godsend. I still managed to pick up articles at Runcorn and was often able to make at least three times profit on my purchase price. Also, some elderly friends of mine, who were retiring to smaller houses in the country, had small pieces of furniture and china, which I might like to buy. There was a small room on the landing with shelves, probably for linen, and I decided to store my antiques there and have them on display when friends came to the house. This became a very popular room and I did a roaring trade with my bridge-playing friends who remember it affectionately to this day, long after we left the house.

John still went looking for work. He was rather a pathetic figure as I saw him walk down the drive in his mackintosh and cap and walk through the gate onto Tarvin Road to catch a bus to Chester. I never let my friends know he was out of work and they would hardly suspect this when they met him because he continued to behave and talk as if he were fully employed. I had to support him in this charade if only to bolster his self esteem and, to a certain extent, my own. I was covering for him all the time.

Worried financially, I at last had an idea. Mother had been left comfortably off by Dad in his will but she was not able to touch the capital which had been left to us five children. I approached the Trustees, after discussing it with Mum, and asked if I could borrow from my future share in the estate to pay for Vicki's school fees. The only snag, as far as I was concerned, was that when I was old and unable to work any more I would have forfeited my income.

I expected John might inherit something from his father. We used to stay sometimes in their lovely old converted farmhouse in Brecon. My mother-in-law was dead and my father-in-law lived with his second son Jim, who was unmarried. He was Managing Director of a roofing firm in mid Wales. The youngest son, Stan, was a Bank Manager so, on the rare occasions that business was discussed, of course John tried his best to hold his own by implying that he was doing very well. At times I felt like jumping up and shouting "*It's not true, it's not true*", but it would have put John in an unenviable position. I would have felt I was letting him down.

My father-in-law, I'm afraid, would not have wanted to hear of John's failure in business. He had a reputation of being 'too lazy to shiver when he was cold'. He had always been comfortably off when they lived in Nicholaston Hall, Gower, and he had retired early. As it happened, John predeceased his father so the Rocke estate went to the two younger boys. At the time it was all speculation as to whether John would inherit anything from his father and I had far more immediate pressing problems to solve.

At Easter we went to Llangernyw for Vicki's half term. The azaleas below the terrace were in full flower and there were thousands of daffodils up the drive and primroses all on the banks of the stream in the valley. It was exactly the environment in which we wanted to see Vicki develop during her most formative years. There was a happy atmosphere amongst the girls and staff too. We always enjoyed our visits. When I got home my mind was made up. What was the good of worrying about my future, it was an unknown quantity anyway. I rang the Trustees and they agreed to pay her school fees from my estate.

CHAPTER 11

I had just returned home from teaching one morning and the phone rang. The call came from the Wallasey Cottage Hospital to say that my brother had been involved in a car accident. He wasn't seriously hurt but they would like to see me. I had some lunch and prepared vegetables for John and me for supper. I left a note saying I hoped to be back about 5.30 p.m.

When I went into the ward and saw Joni he was sitting up with an expression as if 'butter wouldn't melt in his mouth'. *"Joni"*, I said, *"what on earth have you been up to?"*. I could see he wasn't badly hurt and knew he had been drinking far too much during the last year. As he gave no reply I asked one of the nurses.

He had been brought in unconscious, having been found slumped over the steering wheel of his car which had run into the back of a stationary bus. *"He's just had a knock on the head and should be able to go home in a few days"*. I wondered he hadn't been breathalysed but heard since, whether fact or fiction, that you cannot breathalyse an unconscious person.

Reading between the lines I guessed what had happened. I rang the Wallasey police and asked them to collect the car off the road as it could be a hazard at night, unattended and unlit. I went over to see him when he returned to his flat. He had managed to persuade the ambulance men to stop at a wine shop on his way home to purchase a bottle of whisky. *"Just medicinal,"* he explained with his usual charm that even a hardened paramedic could not resist.

As his front door was always unlocked I went in and walked down the long corridor to his sitting room and opened the door. *"Oh Joanie"*, he smiled with delight, *"How lovely to see you"* and, clutching a glass of whisky, he leapt up to give me a hug.

I looked searchingly at my brother. As long as I had known him he had always been jocular, full of good spirits and boundless energy.

I thought of our childhood, happy memories and how we had lain together on the bank of the river in Pennant Valley tickling trout before going into the farmhouse for our birthday teas. I thought of our forays into the old mine shafts, Mini, Pye, Joni and I holding hands till we emerged into the sunlight of the quarry; of skimming slates into the turquoise blue water; of climbing Snowdon on Boxing Day in deep snow with a bottle of Drambuie to drink on the summit.

All those and many other escapades crowded into my mind as I sat looking at him. He had joined the army when he was 21, had been badly wounded when he was 24, had come to terms with his disability only to suffer a serious heart attack. Now he looked a shadow of his former self. His cheerfulness was but a façade to hide his real feelings. Aged about 38 he was no longer able to work.

Frustrated with his stiff leg and damaged heart he had had to give up playing hockey with the Oxton Hockey Club, and climbing in Snowdonia. Most of his young sailing friends were now married which rubbed salt into his wounds because he felt he had nothing to offer a girl in his poor state of health. In his loneliness he had turned to whisky for consolation.

It broke my heart to see the way he was going. I had no right to criticise him but thanked God that Dad was not alive to see him now. As soon as Mum was living with us I would have him to stay. Thank goodness he could still drive his car. It can't have been easy with a straight leg but he never complained.

Back at home, as the weather had improved, I decided I must try and get the herbaceous plants in. I had ordered a load of manure from the farm behind our house so I forked over the soil. The manure was dumped at our gate so I went to look for John to ask him to help me cart it up to the border. I found him at the bottom of the garden near the fields, the whole of this area was still covered with willow herb.

He had cleared a little patch about a yard square and was trying to plant some seeds. *"What are you doing?"* I enquired with dismay. *"I was wondering if you would help me to cart the manure from the gate up to the border"*. He turned a little towards me and said *"Go away, I want to play"*. *"But Johnny"*, I said, *"nothing will grow there, it is too weedy"*. He said nothing. So I went down to the gate and started to load the manure onto a wheelbarrow.

Mother rang to say her house had been sold and would I arrange a date with her when it would be convenient for the furniture van to collect. I wasn't really ready for Mum to come. I had had so much to do I wanted a breathing space before contemplating the burden of another move. For one thing it would be better for us to have all the carpeting moved from The Hollies and re-laid at Harlow before the furniture arrived. Mother agreed, and about two weeks later they were taken up and delivered to my house where I had arranged for a carpet fitter to attend. There was so much stair carpeting that it not only covered our house, but Joni's flat as well.

The Donegal carpet was laid in the dining room. The cream coloured carpet from Mother's sitting room was more than big enough to cover the study room we had allotted for Mother's bedroom. The old rose pink carpet and my carpet had yet to be stitched together for the sitting room which was now looking very pretty with the silvery pink wall paper and white paint work.

At the weekend I met Joni at The Hollies and we went from room to room to see if there were any more pieces he would like to have before the move. Mini was living in America and Nora and Pye had no room for any more furniture. Anyway, everything that came to my house was not mine but would be kept in safe-keeping till Mother died. Joni and I tried to eliminate some of the articles in the attics but Mother wouldn't hear of it. Nothing must be thrown away. There was a large oval galvanized tub with a lid which I objected to. Mother was adamant, *"That tub,"* she said, *"went all the way to America and back when we were children. It was our bathtub"*.

Grandfather had established the first teaching Art School in Boston, Massachusetts. He had twelve children and Mother was next to the youngest. So the bathtub had to come along with all the old trunks, hockey and lacrosse sticks, tennis rackets, netting and tennis posts, fishing rods, shrimping nets, buckets and surf boards and much more from our childhood, long stored in the attic. Well, at least we had the stable block and two sheds to store things in, though one shed was full of things such as our dismantled garden shed which we had not had time to erect. When we did, two years later, we found the door had been left behind in the furniture van and we had to have another made.

We had had a new gas fire fitted in Mother's living room-cum-bedroom and I had washed the fitted cushion on the window seat. The room looked welcoming with the afternoon sun pouring in and cows could be seen over the hedge in the field that ran down the side of the garden. Each time I had been over to Mother I had brought a couple of gilt framed pictures back with me in order to save them from being damaged in the furniture van.

On the removal day I went over to Oxton to be with Mum and to see that nothing was left behind. Joni came over too, to help and supervise the removal of the valuable pieces of furniture. All round the hall was a shelf on which Chinese blue and white dishes and vases were displayed. The housemaid's pantry was also lined with cupboards in which Mother's best china was kept. All these pieces had to be carefully wrapped and packed into crates. I had no idea when we would find time to unpack them but the removal men said we could keep the crates for about six weeks. It was just as well that the firm had sent six men to deal with removing the furniture as it took all six of them to carry the eighteenth century oak dining room table with the heavy bulbous legs into the house.

How we had played under that table when we were very little, sitting on the wooden foot rest. As we got older we used it for table tennis and, of course, it was used every day for all our meals. At Christmas, with relatives staying and the table laden with holly, crackers and nuts, we watched Dad as he carved the huge turkey at one end and passed the plates up to Mother who dispensed the vegetables. When the Aunts and Uncles and my parents had retired to the sitting room, we played party games and Racing Demon till it was time for tea and Christmas cake. Now the table sat in the centre of our dining room resting on the old Donegal carpet and with Mother's armchair at the top end.

All the furniture from Mother's sitting room, which went into ours, was covered in off-white linen patterned with bunches of flowers in shades of pink, lavender and dark purple. It went beautifully with the old rose carpet. Dad's collection of oil paintings was hung in the dining room, hall and sitting room to which my two sea-scapes, bought from Black Diamond Street, were added. Our sitting room furniture went into The Den with the television and became a permanent haven for our PG and us.

Mother was delighted with her room. She had, besides her bed, the large mahogany wardrobe, partly fitted with sliding shelves, drawers below and hanging space on each side; her dressing table, her winged chair and footstool with a trolley beside for books etc., a screen by her bed and finally, her American organ below the small window that looked onto the lawn at the back of the house. With her favourite pictures and pieces of china on the mantelpiece, she felt at home. I always saw she had fresh flowers on the dressing table.

One day, when Vicki was home for half term, I took her to see a large water colour displayed in one of the Watergate Street antique shops as I was contemplating purchasing it but felt I needed a bit of support. As we pulled up at the kerb opposite the shop, Vicki wound down the window to have a clearer view of the picture propped on an easel. The view depicted a lake with cattle in the water and mountains behind. As Vicki wound the window down, a man on the pavement crossed and spoke to her, asking if we needed any help with directions. I replied, *"No thank you, we were just trying to get a better view of a picture in the shop window"*.

I decided to go into the shop and ask the price. Feeling that the painting was worth more than the asking price, I decided to buy it. When I returned to the car the man, who was still talking to Vicki, turned and asked me if I was interested in buying paintings. When I replied, *"Well it depends on the artist and the subject,"* he said, *"Well I have a large seascape at home which was left to me by a friend and I would like to sell it but I don't know the name of the artist"*. *"Where do you live?"* I asked him and he replied that he had a flat in Chester and gave me the address. I said I would call that evening.

After he had gone I realised I knew nothing about the man or the respectability of the flats. Fortunately, one of Vicki's old form mistresses lived there so I contacted her and she reassured me that I had nothing to fear as she knew the man in question.

That evening I duly turned up on time and the man took me into his flat where a large oil painting hung on the wall behind the door. The paint was very dark and the canvas badly torn but on the frame I saw the name Clarkson Stansfield. My heart leapt as I knew the artist to be a well known marine painter. *"What do you want for it?"* I asked. *"Anything you like to give me,"* he replied. *"Would £10 do?"* I enquired hesitantly, *"That's fine,"* he said.

It had a heavy gilt frame so he took it down to my car and put it in the boot. I knew I couldn't possibly restore it as the canvas needed re-lining and in its badly damaged state I had no idea of its true value or if I could even re-sell it, but I was sure I could make some profit on the sale and I was excited about having even the temporary ownership of a painting by such a well known artist.

When a doctor friend of ours, who was a collector, offered me £100 for the painting I reluctantly agreed after discussing it with my family. The money would be very helpful, as Martin's school fees at Sedbergh were £350 a term. Though he was due to leave soon, I just couldn't afford to turn down the offer.

With Mother settled in there seemed to be very little time for decorating. I knew I would have to give my tutoring job up in the near future. I continued to write articles for Cheshire Life, Yorkshire Illustrated and The Dalesman but they took a lot of preparation which, in a way, I found therapeutic. My real source of income came from my trading with antiques. Though my monthly articles for Deesider had finished I had found in the back streets of Rock Ferry, Birkenhead and Wallasey a rich hunting ground and, somehow, I found time to visit them at least once a month.

Mother, though chair-ridden, was very undemanding. She would not have television but had a radio and, as long as she had her tapestry or some article of sewing to do, she was happy. John would sit with her often in the evenings. She was very fond of him and never enquired about his work.

Out of deference to Mother we decided to change the

name of the house to Hollinsclose. Mother had been born in Hollinsclose Hall in Bradford and as the garden in front was full of holly trees it seemed very appropriate. Mother was delighted.

The lawn at the back of the house had been kept cut when the house was empty so it was not too difficult to mow with our old mower. We set up the old tennis posts and net and just managed to erect enough netting at the field end. I managed to get a second hand line marker from Hayes Sale room. We decided to give up our membership of the Hough Green Tennis Club but continued to hunt with the Royal Rock Beagles in the winter months which we all enjoyed so much, especially as John and Martin were both whips; though Martin could only whip-in during the Christmas holiday.

* * * * *

The Royal Rock Beagle Hunt was founded in 1845 by a few gentlemen resident in Rock Ferry, Birkenhead. They met at the house of Rev. Christopher Ranson, to form a subscription pack of Beagles for the purpose of hunting hounds over the Hundred of Wirral. It is the oldest pack in the country.

Hunting with John and the children was, for me, a. wonderful way of relaxing and leaving all my worries behind. There is a particular friendship which is to be found amongst the hunting fraternity and country lovers which is born from the pleasure of running with one's friends, in every kind of weather and watching the hounds working. There is much etiquette to be learnt in the hunting field too, making an excellent training ground for young children. At the end of the day's hunting tea was usually provided at a member's house.

Between the years 1939-45 hunting was disbanded, as war had been declared and the Master and most of the members had joined the forces.

The Hunt was re-formed in 1947 under the joint mastership of P. D. Stevenson and J. V. Kelly. When I first joined the Hunt, before I was married, we met at most of the Wirral villages. I feel I know every field between Oxton and Shotwick. We met at Raby Mere, Landican, Puddington, Capenhurst, Badgers Rake, Raby and Dunkirk. On a Meet Card dated 1948 we met at The Wheatsheaf, Raby, The Yacht Inn, Woodbank, Great Sutton, Gayton, Backford Cross, Willaston Mill and Storeton. We hunted along the marshes of the Dee. We also met in Wales on Moel Arthur and at the home of Sir Brian Robertson at Pale Gates, Llanderfel, where we all played football on the terrace after tea!

In the years when Col. King was Master in 1853, Wirral was a very rural place in which to hunt. In living memory many of the great estates have ceased to exist, the building of the railways imperilled the lives of hunting hounds and the building of the Manchester Ship Canal lost for ever fine hunting grounds around Bromborough and Ellesmere Port. The increase of population and the spread of towns such as Birkenhead, have swallowed up vast areas of beautiful countryside in the North end of Wirral and we hunted no more at Wallasey, Seacombe, Bebington, Tranmere, Moreton and Upton.

With the building of the M53 motorway it became impossible to hunt hounds with safety and the hounds were re-kennelled in the Vale of Clwyd in Wales.

* * * * *

Vicki at the Royal Rock Beagles Puppy Show in 1965

At the weekends, John did what he could in the garden. He was a very good hedge cutter and enjoyed mowing the lawn. Half the front of the house was covered with a very neglected overgrown ivy. He cut the whole of this away, clipping everything off tight to the thread-like stems which covered the brickwork. In the spring the ivy glistened with the tiny fresh green leaves of the new growth. I had bought about a dozen Madonna lily bulbs from our house in Hoole and I planted them in a bed in front of the dining room window. The sill was only about eighteen inches from the ground so I thought they would look lovely in that position, and they did.

My friend, Issie, whom I had met in France years ago, sent me half a dozen roses for the long rose beds and another friend gave me four shrub roses. As we now had all the furniture in the house and had called a truce on decorating, we concentrated on improving the garden and getting rid of the willow herb. John sprayed the whole area and we came across pathways and dozens of rope edging stones scattered about which we collected and replaced. We could then get a better idea of the original lay-out of the garden.

There were also a lot of very old and sometimes rotten fruit trees in the orchard that would have to come down. We had four huge pear trees, a Victoria plum, two or three damsons and at least a dozen varieties of apple. They had been planted in four long rows interspersed with gooseberry bushes and raspberry canes, now much mildewed, but, by cutting out the old canes and pruning the gooseberry bushes, I had a better crop the next year and made pies and jams - but the apples defeated us. We picked the best for the apple store but there were thousands more to be collected and given away.

Joni had again been invited to sail on the Sail Training Ship, the Winston Churchill. He had been awarded a Master's Certificate for his knowledge of seamanship and his strict discipline with the young crew. Mother wanted so much to see him on board as the ship was docked in Birkenhead. It caused her great pain to walk from her room down the hall and into the waiting car in the drive. When we arrived at the dockside we were able to drive the car alongside the ship and were level with the deck where Joni was leaning on the ship's rail to welcome us. It was a supreme moment of pleasure for Mother.

Next time he came to stay with us I decided I must have a serious talk about the way that he not only left his front door unlocked at night but often open where it could be seen from the road below. I also knew he was having trouble with the War Office. Having been invalided out of the army and suffering a further serious heart attack he should have been able to claim a pension but, as his doctor would have been consulted, I suspected he might have mentioned his alcoholism. The W.O. might feel, therefore, that if he were to give up drinking and smoking (he was a chain smoker) he could be fit enough to take up some part time job as he was still comparatively young. I knew he had been turned down after his last medical.

One weekend when we were all working in the garden John kept going back to the house for a glass of water. "*You seem to be very thirsty*" I commented. "*Yes*", he said, "*I am*". We decided to have some tea but it didn't really quench his thirst. On Monday he decided to go and see his doctor who told him he would have to go to the hospital for a check up. There it was confirmed that he had bronze diabetes and would need to go into hospital for a few days to be stabilised and learn how to give himself injections. Poor John, he hated having to do this and quite often forgot, with disastrous results.

I woke in the night once to find him standing in the middle of the room with a fixed expression on his face. I went up to him and asked him, "*Why are you standing there?"* and tried to push him back to bed but he resisted violently. It was about 3 o'clock in the morning but I rang the doctor who said he would be over as soon as possible. In the meantime with much struggling, I managed to force him back onto the bed where he lay staring up at the ceiling.

When the doctor arrived I took him straight up to the bedroom. He looked down at John, *"You haven't been giving yourself your injections,"* he admonished. John did not react and appeared not even to notice the doctor standing there. He turned to me and said, *"Will you please bring me some sugar and a tea spoon".* Having been supplied with these, he endeavoured to force some sugar between John's clenched teeth. It took some time to accomplish this and much sugar was spilt all over the bedclothes. At last John's eyes began to focus normally and he looked enquiringly at the doctor. Robin repeated his earlier remark and John, now sitting up had to confess that he had indeed forgotten.

I saw Robin down to the front door and asked him, *"Will he be alright in the morning?"* *"Yes, he won't suffer any ill effects, but do try to impress upon him the necessity of having his insulin injections each day and give him some sugar lumps to keep in his pocket in case he feels unwell when he is out".* To a certain extent John had now to be on a strict diet, no sweet puddings or jams etc. From when we were first married I had noticed rusty coloured markings on his legs. He said he had shown them to an army doctor during the war when he was in Bombay but he was told they were sunburn patches on his very fair skin. In fact they were a sign of bronze diabetes. Perhaps the diabetes was the reason for his lethargy and with treatment his health might improve. Sadly, it was to prove otherwise.

CHAPTER 12

John had always been a very good driver and I loved being driven by him but now there were problems. Occasionally, he would swerve the car for no apparent reason and when I looked at him I saw that his eyelids were drooping and he was obviously having difficulty keeping his eyes open. *"John,"* I remonstrated *"don't go to sleep. Would you like me to take over the driving?"* *"I am not going to sleep,"* he replied hotly. *"Well you were closing your eyes"*. *"Rubbish,"* he remarked, but I kept watching him all the time and every time I saw his eyes closing I talked to him forcing him to concentrate.

Allowing him to drive, however, became a nightmare. When I told him I wanted to take over the driving the next time we went out together he became very angry.

So I made an appointment with his doctor and told him about it, begging him to stop him driving. He replied that there should be no need at all for him to be like this if he was taking his insulin daily.

However, the crunch came one day when we were returning from a meet of the Beagles and Martin was in the back of the car. John was driving fairly fast and started to drive straight towards the back of a stationary bus. I shouted to him to stop and he swerved away at the last moment indignantly blaming me for nearly causing an accident. I looked into the back of the car and saw Martin huddled up on the floor behind one of the seats. When we arrived home I spoke to Martin about it. I had mentioned John's erratic driving to him before but as he had not then experienced it I think he thought I was exaggerating. *"Well, I know something."* he said, *"I won't go in the car again with Dad driving"*.

So for the safety of all of us I had to make the horrible decision of hiding the car keys and not allowing him to drive. Naturally he was furious. As diplomatically as I could I explained my reason but he refused to listen. Vicki also confirmed my fears as she had been picked up by him from a party and had been terrified on the drive home.

The sad fact was that gradually his authority had been taken away from him. For years I had to pay all the bills for gas, water, electricity, clothes and food as they were left unpaid. If they were long overdue a representative from the company would call at the house and with some embarrassment present me with an account. Apologising for my husband's forgetfulness, I wrote the cheque. I hated having to do this because I knew it must cause John resentment. He must have felt hopelessly inadequate and helpless.

At my wit's end, a friend advised me to go and talk to a Canon, I cannot remember his name, who was vicar of St. John's church in Chester, as he was a well-known counsellor.

I made an appointment and when I got to the church, instead of taking me into the vestry where I could have spoken to him in private, he came and stood at the end of the pew where I was sitting and, as he was a very tall man it was difficult speaking to him in a quiet voice when visitors to the church were walking past us all the time. When I had told him about all my problems he just said, "*Well I think it's a very sad story*". As he had no more to say I got up and walked out of the church.

John had an appointment with the diabetic specialist who confirmed that the dosage prescribed by the doctor was correct but, as he was often seen to be rubbing his chest, the doctor sent him to the Infirmary for an X-ray. There they found his liver was enlarged and for treatment he had to go twice a week to the Infirmary to have a pint of blood taken away. Curiously this seemed to have no ill effect on him, but I insisted on taking him in the car.

Poor John, barred from driving the car, it must have been the last straw. I couldn't risk it any longer; but when we went to take Vicki out from school for the day he made my life a misery. He continually criticised my driving, accusing me of driving into the kerb etc. I knew why he was behaving like this and just had to ignore it. By the time we had collected Vicki, his resentment had vanished and we always had a happy day together, often having a picnic by the river in the summer.

Martin had now left Sedbergh and was working with the River Board. When Vicki left Hafodunos we suggested she took a shorthand and typing course as, whatever career she decided upon, being able to type was an asset.

After an evening meal I often went and sat with Mother as she was alone most of the day, though I had my lunch with her whenever I could. This became an extra strain on me as I was torn between being with her and wanting to be with the family in the Den where we could watch television and catch up on the day's news. Vicki by now had taken a job with Beresford Adams Estate Agents in Chester.

I was also becoming increasingly concerned about Joni's irresponsible behaviour. He was now drinking the best part of a bottle of whisky a day. His flat had become terribly neglected, with piles of empty food tins left on the kitchen table which he was too lazy to take down the long flight of stairs to the bins.

I went over to see him and was horrified to see that he had sold the 17th century beautiful dark oak dresser that had come from our home in Oxton and which Mother had given to him. In its place stood an ugly Victorian piece. *"Oh Joni, Joni what are you doing?"* I groaned. Due to his habit of leaving his front door open at night, I knew he had all sorts of odd people walking in and someone must have told a dealer. It was useless asking him about it because I knew he had sold it to get money to buy whisky.

I had brought a picnic lunch and he was so pathetically grateful, saying it was the best meal he had had for ages. Fearful for the valuable oil painting he had I tackled him again about leaving the front door open at night. *"Anyone could walk in,"* I warned him, *"and attack you"*. He became truculent and said, balling his fists, *"I'm not worried, I could fight them"*. I asked him if he had had any luck with the medical board and he said he hoped to hear from them soon.

He chain smoked all day and the ash and stubs from his cigarettes were piled about two foot high on the floor by his armchair in which he now slept at night. Although his doctor had told him he must go for a walk every day, I knew his leg pained him.

He had some very good friends opposite whose dog he took out for a walk. They rang me one day to say that Joni had a sort of circus rider living with him and he was keeping his horse in the front garden!

I was horrified because the owners of the bottom flat had to walk past this horse to get to their front door. Also when John was out this man could steal anything and possibly run up an enormous telephone bill. Besides, this was a very respectable residential area and the garden, with a large rockery and gorse bushes, wasn't suitable for a horse to live in.

I rang Joni at once but as usual he laughed it all off. Then the inevitable happened, he was admitted into hospital with a small heart attack. He was there for about a month during which time the circus chap blocked all the front garden off with any old fences or planks of wood he could find to stop his horse jumping over the wall.

When Joni returned to the flat he realised what an appalling mess the man had made of the garden and asked him to leave. I'll say this for him, he may have caused outrage to the local inhabitants, but he never stole anything.

At last Joni was awarded his army pension. This made an enormous difference to him mentally and physically. As he had been unable to work he only had the money Mother provided to live on. Now he had a man from Social Services two days a week to help him and do his shopping etc.

Together they transformed his very neglected rooms,

repainting the walls of his kitchen, corridor and bedroom. All the cream paintwork was washed in his sitting room and the old oak table polished every week. Joni bought some special polish to treat the eight beautifully embossed leather chairs which he had sadly neglected. Seeing his home help twice a week gave Joni something to look forward to and, as spring came, we all tackled the overgrown front garden and rockery which we filled with nasturtiums. He bought a mower for the front lawn and his help cut the grass every week. In fact, he often returned in the evenings to work in the garden or help clean out an old greenhouse in which Joni decided to grow salads and tomatoes.

It was a joy to see him so much happier when I visited him and he took me down to the greenhouse to inspect his tomatoes. In the winter months he came and stayed with us frequently. He could spend time with Mother, and John, Martin and Vicki were always delighted to see him when they would reminisce about fishing at Llangernyw and climbing in Snowdonia.

John had been rubbing his side again and I persuaded him to see the doctor who sent him for more X-rays.

One morning I was sitting on the cushions on the windowsill of Mum's room when the phone rang. It was my cousin Tom Blackburn on the phone from Yorkshire, saying they were on a touring holiday and wanted to visit Chester the following day, so I immediately invited them all to lunch. We looked forward to seeing them as they rarely came into Cheshire.

I started at once by setting the table for nine of us, Mother, John, and myself, Martin, Vicki, Tom and Edwina and their two children, Tommy and Charlotte. I arranged a bowl of flowers from the garden in the centre of the table and then went to the shops to buy all the food I would need for our meal. I prepared a caramel custard so that it would be set for the following day.

The following morning I prepared all the vegetables and placed two well-larded chickens in the baking tray ready for roasting. I had decided to cook the stuffing separately. Then I prepared the bread sauce with plenty of pepper and salt and grated onion.

The kitchen was grand to work in as the coke stove was always kept alight in the winter and I had the big kitchen table in the centre of the room to work on. Apple pie was always a favourite with the menfolk and I had plenty of apples in store.

I was starting to make the pastry when the phone rang. It was John's doctor, "*I am sorry,*" he said, "*but we have had the results of John's X-ray which we had sent to King's College Hospital in London. Has John made his will?*" I felt as though my whole body had turned to water. "*What do you mean?*" I stammered. "*Don't press me*", he replied, "*you should be hearing from the specialist at King's College in a few days*".

I put down the receiver. For some minutes I don't even know what I did. Then the full implication of the doctor's words sunk in. I threw the pastry back into the bowl and somehow managed to stagger round the hall to Mother's room where I collapsed on the window seat sobbing. "*John's dying*", I said. Mother turned to me and in a shocked voice said, "*Oh, don't say that, Joanie, what do you mean?*" I repeated the conversation I had had with the doctor over the phone. She tried her best to comfort me. *"Where is John at the moment?"* *"I think he is pottering round the garden - I don't know,"* I replied in distress.

Somehow I knew that I had to pull myself together as the Blackburn's were arriving in about three hours and I was unable to contact them; also I had to show no sign of my distress to John who, thank God, appeared to be unaware of the seriousness of his condition. I started again to try and make the pastry but I could not concentrate and shaking and sobbing I threw it all into the sink and cried myself out.

I managed to make myself a cup of tea and took two aspirins and quieter now, I could only think of John. On no account should he have any suspicion that anything was wrong. This fact must sustain me all day, however sick at heart I felt. Nor must I tell any of the family yet. Trembling with emotion I made the pastry again and chopped up the apples. I collected the glasses for the sherry when they arrived and placed them on the dumb waiter in the long sitting room.

The fire had already been lit. Later, I would ask Martin to help Mother to walk from her room and sit her in a comfy chair by the fire. I went into Mother's room and begged her not to mention the conversation I had had with the doctor to anyone. *"Perhaps, Joanie,"* she said, *"when you get John to London they will be able to treat him"*.

I went upstairs to change, John was in the room washing his hands. *"Johnny"*, I said, *"I've put the drinks in the sitting room so will you cope with that for me and have a look at the fire?"* *"Yes"*, he said quietly, *"I'll go down now"*. John was teetotal so why, in God's name, should he of all people have an enlarged liver, and what did it mean?

When they were all settled and chatting happily to Mother, Edwina came out to the kitchen to help me dishing up the meal. I longed to tell her about John, but thought better of it. I had only met her once before at her wedding.

When I returned to the sitting room, Tom, John, Martin and Tommy were all discussing the fishing on the Wharfe and in my mind's eye I saw my beloved green fields and woods of Grasssington where we had roamed and been so happy and the memory caused me such agonies of distress that I felt the pain would stifle me. *"I'll just get the white sauce on,"* I said as I left the room, *"and then I think we are all ready to eat."*

The Blackburn's left about 5.30 and, after supper that evening, everyone went into the Den to watch television. I took some tea into Mother's room and soon after crept up to bed, my headache now being so severe that aspirins didn't alleviate the pain. I pressed my forehead into the cool pillow and prayed something could be done for John when we went to London. He came up to bed soon after and, as he slid in beside me, the hot tears poured down my face into the pillow.

The next few days were a nightmare. John sat in the Den a lot and sometimes when I saw him rubbing his side I asked him if it hurt and he said, *"No, but it seems very stiff and swollen"*. *"The doctor suggests you go to King's College Hospital for treatment and I am waiting to hear from them. If they want you to go I will drive you down"*.

Dreadfully anxious, after waiting two days I decided to ring up the Hospital and ask to speak to the specialist who had seen John's X-rays.

I contacted the Hospital and asked if I could speak to the specialist whose name I had obtained from John's doctor. I was told he was on his rounds on a ward. *"Will you please ask him to come to the phone,"* I begged, *"It is urgent,"* and I gave my name. I heard a man saying, *"Yes?"* I told him I was ringing about my husband and had been given to understand he needed urgent treatment.

There was a short silence then the voice said, *"I'm sorry, I don't remember the name and as my secretary is off at present I can't find anything".*

Frustrated rage overtook me. *"Mr Lee,"* I said, *"you saw the X-rays of my husband this week and now you say you cannot find them. It was on your assessment of them that you rang my doctor, who then rang me to tell me my husband was dying. Will you please do something?"* *"Just a minute"*, he replied and when he returned to the phone he said quietly, *"Will you bring your husband up to King's as soon as possible".*

I was still stunned by the blunt and insensitive words of my doctor on the phone as at no time had he implied that John's condition was life threatening. I suppose I was in a state of shock, but plans had to be made for Mother to be cared for as I had no idea how long I would be away in London. I rang my sister Nora and asked if she could come and she readily agreed.

The day after the luncheon party I went into Martin's bedroom to tell him about John. I sat on his bed and said, *"Martin, I'm afraid Dad is dying,"* and I told him everything the doctor had said to me on the phone. I told

Vicki a few days later when I knew we were going to London and begged them to be cheerful and encouraging when we left.

When the day came for us to leave I made sandwiches and filled a Thermos. With a sickening feeling in my stomach we set off. I knew very well that this was probably the last picnic we would ever have together. Feeling desperately lonely and unhappy,

I had rung a very old friend of mine who had gone to live in Haslemere, Surrey, to ask if I could spend the night with her. I had no idea how far it would be and I had never driven in London before. All I knew was that I hadn't the money to stay in London and I wanted, that night of all nights, to be with a friend.

With great difficulty I managed to get through Hyde Park Corner and on to King's College Hospital. John was taken up to a ward and told to undress and get into bed when the Doctor would come and see him. At that time it hadn't occurred to me that I would be leaving the hospital in the dark. It was early April.

A nurse asked me to follow her. I was taken to a private room where the specialist who had seen John's X-rays was waiting to speak to me. He told me very kindly' that nothing could be done for John as he had a very rare condition called haemachromatosis and that it was congenital. He had only a few weeks to live.

"If you knew nothing could be done for him why did you ask me to bring him to London? He could have died at home with his family around him. Please could I take him home, by ambulance if necessary," I pleaded. He just

117

shook his head. Had I not been so utterly exhausted, I might have fought harder, but I had reached the limit of my endurance. I had hardly slept for three weeks, my hair hung like grey string, I could not cry any more.

So this was the answer to the mystery of John's increasing deterioration of health which I had witnessed from the early days of our marriage and, because of which, our family doctor in his ignorance of this rare condition, had later accused John of malingering. It was a bitter pill and too late to heap blame on the doctors who had been responsible for John's health.

Apparently the condition was so rare that it was not immediately identified and by the time he was receiving some treatment it was too late.

I was consumed with a feeling of helpless rage. I spent the rest of that day with John and left about 5.30. It was now dark and I had no idea which road I should take. I drove back to Hyde Park and drove up a road where I could pull up at the kerb. A car pulled up in front of me and I waved to the driver and opened my passenger window. He came back and I asked him if he could direct me to the road I had been advised to take out of London. He said he was unable to help me.

As it was rush hour there were many people about so I stopped quite a few asking them the same question. As I was in Oxford Street I hoped I might see a policeman. As I wanted to make some progress I just drove on, stopping from time to time to enquire from a pedestrian.

After about an hour's driving I was told I was on the wrong road and should go back. With no street map I was hopelessly lost and about two hours later found myself in Oxford Street again. Frankly, after having the long and stressful journey to London and the talk with the specialist, I was in no state to be driving anyway. I made a U turn in the middle of Oxford Street.

On the outskirts of London at about 10.30 at night I was confronted by a large pub on the right side of the road. In neon lights on the front of the building were the words TAKE COURAGE. Like a shot of adrenalin it freed my lagging spirits to carry on to Haslemere where I arrived at my friend's house at midnight.

For the next fortnight I sat at John's bedside all day. Friends and relatives called and sat with me from time to time, but every day I had this exhausting drive through London and unknown streets to the houses of friends somewhere out of town. The nurses were very kind and brought me cups of tea and some lunch on a tray outside the ward.

On the last day John was taken to a private room. I sat by him holding his hand. He was unconscious and slowly his breathing just stopped. I felt as though mine had stopped too. I went out of the room and told a nurse who came in at once with a doctor.

I was standing by the window and the doctor asked if I was alright. I just nodded and the nurse went to the bed and pulled up the sheet over his head. *"Don't,"* I cried, *"please don't cover him"*. As long as I could see his face I felt part of him as though he were still with me. After a short time the nurse gently took me out of the room and I sat on a chair outside the door.

John died on 26th April 1967. He was 51 years old.

Martin and Vicki had been alerted and came down in Martin's MG the day before and spent the night with friends in London. I arranged that John should come back to Chester and Vicki drove my car home with one hand in mine all the way.

He was buried in Christleton churchyard. Four Whips from the Royal Rock Beagles carried the coffin, Martin, Anthony Hannay, Anthony Harris and Hugh Dagnall.

The flowers were from the garden. When the coffin was carried from the church round to the cemetery for burial, a flight of swallows swooped down and flew over us. A fitting farewell to a beloved countryman.

CHAPTER 13

Some weeks after we returned from London, Vicki came into the kitchen one day and said, *"Mum, would you mind if I went up to London? I am sure it would not be too difficult to get a secretarial job there".* She said she had had a talk with Martin about it because she didn't want me to be on my own, but Martin had assured her that he wanted to stay in Chester. I was delighted because I knew quite a few of her friends had decided to look for work in the capital and I felt it was a chance for her to spread her wings and meet other people.

A friend of hers, Martin Jones, was going down to Law School in Guildford and gave her a lift to London. Vicki found a job and the weekend after she arrived in London, Martin came up to London in his car and drove Vicki round to find a flat. She joined two other girls, one of whom was Jenny Hill.

At home I now spent most of my evenings sitting with Mother. I took in some tea and we played Rummy. Though John and I had done so little together for many years, when he had gone the whole purpose of our married life seemed to have gone too. I felt very desolate.

All those years of worry and stress had for me been mitigated by the thought that when there was no need for us to work any more we could at last be together in a cottage in the country. At no time had John's doctor ever intimated that he was incurably ill.

I somehow continued to run the house, buying in food, cooking meals, automatically. John's Bank Manager told me that John had left only £30 in the Bank. He had no shares or life policy and, as he had not been able to earn a living for many years, I was not eligible for a pension. Although I heard what he said I was too saddened by it all to reply constructively. I already knew that John would be unable to leave me any money as he had not inherited from his family, his father still being alive. For years I had had to manage on what I could earn and, in the latter years, on what Mother contributed to help run the house.

I spent most afternoons writing in reply to the hundreds of kind letter of condolence that we had received. My PG, who had lived with us for fourteen years, had decided to move out into a flat of his own. I did not bother to replace him. Friends called and my dear friend Dorothy Dodd took me to the Cotswolds for a long weekend so, as they say, life goes on - as it must.

One day when I was working in the garden, I saw a young man walking up the drive. I looked at him in amazement. "*Rodney*," I gasped running to give him a hug, "*Where have you come from?*" I had not seen him for many years as he had been working in Kenya.

We had met him as a little boy of seven when we were on holiday in Criccieth, North Wales. He had been sent to stay with his aunt there as he had just lost his Mother who had died of influenza. We knew his aunt well and she contacted us hoping Rodney could join us sometime as he was the same age as Martin. The upshot of it was that the little boy arrived every day after breakfast at our house clutching his bathing trunks and towel and some food to spend all day with us for we had all fallen in love with his cheery smile.

I welcomed him in and we talked all about our families and I asked him what he was doing now. He said he had given up working for Brooke Bond and had taken a temporary job in London whilst looking for permanent work. I told him Vicki was in London and gave him her address.

He called there a few days later and when one of Vicki's flat mates answered the door and shouted up the stairs, *"Vicki, there is someone here to see you called Rodney Jordan,"* she could hardly believe it. Shortly after Vicki and Rodney came up to Chester together and we reminisced about all the happy days at Criccieth so long ago where we swam in the sea and picnicked in Pennant Valley. Back in London Rodney continued to see Vicki.

It must have been about six months after John's death when King's College Hospital contacted me by letter informing me that Martin and Vicki should come to the hospital for certain tests to see if either of them had inherited haemachromatosis, one of the tests being a liver puncture. We were shattered but knew that it had to be faced.

I asked Mother's companion, Mrs Phillips, whom she had had before, if she could come over to look after Mother whilst I went up with Martin to London. Vicki and Jenny had moved from their old flat and were now sharing a flat in Ebury Street. There was a little hotel nearby so, as soon as Mrs Phillips was installed at Hollinsclose, I booked into the hotel to be near Vicki. Martin took me up in his car and stayed with friends. As every day we had appointments at the hospital for tests, Martin picked us both up in the morning.

After some of the tests, which did not take more than a couple of hours, we spent our time sightseeing. There is nothing more destructive than worry, but I could not help feeling anxious and apprehensive. I sat for long hours in a waiting-room for either Martin or Vicki to return. One of the specialists came and talked to me. He said much could be done to control the condition if caught in its early stages. *"The trouble with your husband,"* he explained, *"was that his illness was congenital and continued without treatment for most of his life"*. I was really neither comforted or reassured.

Rodney called every evening at the hotel on his way back from work for a drink and we sat in comfortable armchairs and relaxed. One day both children had to undergo the unpleasant experience of a liver puncture. They stayed in overnight and the following day we were given the 'all clear' on both of them. We returned to the hotel for the now customary evening drink awaiting Rodney to join us. Vicki went to the desk to buy some cigarettes so was not with us when Rodney walked in. He looked around with some alarm, *"Where's Vicki?"* he asked. *"She has just gone to buy some cigarettes,"* I replied. His relief was obvious and from that moment I knew he really cared for her.

Martin drove me back from London and we arrived at about eight in the evening. As soon as we had had something to eat I went in to see Mother to give her the good news that the tests had proved negative. I found Mother apparently asleep in bed and Mrs Phillips told me she had not been feeling at all well but she had given her the little white tablets the doctor has prescribed for her. I was very tired so went up to bed but woke early unable to settle.

I decided to go down to Mother's room to see if she

was still asleep. As soon as I saw her I knew she was dying. She was unconscious and her breathing was irregular. I rang the doctor who came soon after I called him. He said he had rung for an ambulance. Why, why, why, did I let her go?

She probably only had an hour to live and I could have been with her. I think that on these occasions, one is too stunned to think rationally. The ambulance men were there and I stood helplessly while they placed her in a chair to convey her to the ambulance. Immediately they had gone I rang Joni who said he would come over, but by the time he arrived I had heard from the hospital that Mother was dead. I rang Nora and Pye and we all agreed that Mother should be buried in Landican Cemetery, Birkenhead, with Dad. Joni stayed with me till Nora and Pye arrived, so, excepting for Mini who was in America, we were all together to say goodbye to Mum.

I realised that, in the not too distant future, Nora, Pye and Mini would want to come and stay so that Mother's pictures and furniture could be divided equally between us. Mother had not made a will, so I arranged for an antique dealer to come and value all Mother's possessions in the house. They were all listed and priced so that we could have a sheet each on which all the items were individually valued.

When the antique dealer had been valuing Mother's possessions, he walked across the hall looking towards the James Webb oil painting on the opposite wall on each side of which hung the two seascapes; I had bought for two shillings and sixpence each at the shop in Black Diamond Street. I had, in the intervening years, cleaned both paintings and noticed the initials H.R. in the corner of the canvass. He remarked rather enviably, *"You have a pair of valuable Henry Redmore seascapes on that wall*". Some years later, when family money was scarce, I sold them both for just under £3,000 each at Sotheby's.

I felt an enormous responsibility not to touch anything or let the family feel that I had taken anything which did not belong to me before they all came up, so I touched nothing in Mother's room. My home help and I stripped and removed all the bed linen, tidied and dusted all the furniture, then shut the door. I felt her loss terribly. She had been so patient and I fretted that I had not done enough for her.

A few days later Martin and I were washing up the supper plates in the kitchen. We had a rack on the wall in which were slotted all the saucepan lids. As I stretched to put one in the space the whole lot crashed to the ground with a cacophony of sound. I started to scream, covering my face with my hands. Having suffered weeks of tension and the loss of John, the trip to London with the children and Mother's death so soon after, I just snapped. Martin threw the drying cloth down and turned and put his arms round me as the pent-up tears streamed down my face.

It was early summer before we could fix a convenient date for my three sisters to come and stay. A couple of days before, I went into Mother's room to dust and place flowers on her dressing table. As I opened the door and stepped into the room I was horrified to see a powdering of red dust all over part of the furniture in one corner. I knew immediately it was dry rot, having seen it at Mother's house some years before.

I shut the door slowly, not wanting to go in and disturb the spores any more than I could help. It couldn't have come at a worse time. I decided to get in touch with a well known firm of timber specialists and explain my situation. Fortunately, they promised to send someone that afternoon. When he arrived I took him into Mother's room. He hesitated for a few moments and then walked past the large mahogany wardrobe and I heard him jump on the floor. There was the sound of splintering wood and he dropped through a hole into the foundations below the floor. When he reappeared he explained that, *"I had a large fruiting body beneath the floor boards"*.

He got up and went out of the room and into the cloakroom, which was adjacent to Mother's room. After a short time examining the much-mended old pipes he said, *"Here is the source of the dry rot. These old pipes have probably been leaking for some time into the wall next to the bedroom"*. I was elated and said, *"Will you please mention that in your report which I will send to my Insurance Co, for I had insured the house against damage from leaking pipes"*. This he promised to do and I was much relieved. I wanted the repairs done as soon as possible for fear of the spores spreading and he arranged to come the week after the family had left. He took a sample of the Victorian skirting board with him as he left, to enable him to make a match. I Hoovered away as much as I could of the red dust and placed a piece of board over the splintered hole.

Min arrived from America and Nora and Pye from Chesham and Bideford. I told them about the dry rot and that I didn't want them to walk all over the room as there were spores everywhere. We decided to leave one of the windows open on to the window seat inside so that they could come into the room that way and cause the least disturbance.

I said I would not go in with them. I could never have gone through Mother's personal possessions so soon after her death. I did not touch her desk and dressing table. It was different for me, as I had looked after her for twelve years. No doubt my sisters felt I would have helped myself before they came up but at that stage it would have felt like stealing. I had never opened Mother's desk or dressing table drawers and I couldn't do it now. Nora found a lot of notes and paper cuttings about Grandfather and included them in a book she wrote about his life in America. Joni joined us for supper and the following day we all sat round the dining room table with the lists, prepared by the valuer, of Mother's possessions in the house. We took it in turns to choose bearing in mind the value of the piece so that we more or less had a fair share each.

As the weather was lovely we put rugs on the lawn beneath the beech tree and had tea. Min had numerous phone calls to America, arranging the transport and packing of furniture, pictures and porcelain and over the next few days Nora and Pye arranged for their pieces of furniture to be collected.

Seeing the paintings being taken off the wall distressed me the most. The gaps that were left contribute to my feeling of recent loss of Mother and John. A few months later there was a house sale down our road and I bought, very cheaply, two large water-colours which I hung in the sitting room.

CHAPTER 14

With the loss of Mother I had much more time to concentrate on all the things I wanted to do. I could garden all day if I felt like it or spend hours hunting round the antique shops searching for bargains. On a fine day I sometimes drove to Wirral to make sketches for future watercolour painting of Burton or Shotwick villages which I was able to finish at home. I could spend a whole morning at the Records Office in Chester researching the hundreds of books on Cheshire or any other subject for facts to complete an article for the Wirral Journal or Cheshire Life.

Fortunately, Martin was very rarely away at night and there was much to keep me occupied in the daytime. The timber repair firm came soon after my sisters had returned home and did an excellent job, perfectly matching the high Victorian skirting board with the new wood. I was given a certificate of proof that all the dry rot had been eradicated and my insurance company paid the bill with a proviso that I replaced the old lead pipes in the cloakroom.

Joni came over frequently to stay with us. It was a joy to have him and a comfort to Martin and me because he had been very fond of John and missed him as much as we did as their temperaments had been well matched. They had fished, sailed and climbed mountains together with a little poaching thrown in for good measure in some isolated mountain lake.

When the weather was fine I packed up a picnic for us

both often consisting of hard-boiled eggs, spring onions from the garden, rolls and butter, cheese and Mars Bars. We also took a Thermos of tea to wash it all down to which Joni added a liberal dash of whisky.

Our favourite drive was to Llangernyw in North Wales and we sat by the river where Dad, John and he had fished together on many occasions and where I could remember Vicki standing on the bridge in her school uniform with John's arm round her shoulder. So many happy memories which Joni and I could enjoy together, though I had to fight back the tears knowing how much Johnny would love to have been with us.

All our lives we had been inveterate mushroom gatherers and in late summer we collected a basket-full from the fields and fried them for breakfast with bacon and fresh eggs and honey from farms and filled the boot of the car with fallen wood. When Martin came home from work we had supper round the kitchen table and then retired to the Den to watch television or just reminisce, mostly about fishing. For the first time since the war I was able to relax.

Though I still had to earn enough money to pay the bills the immediate pressure was off. Vicki was in London and enjoying Rodney's company. From time to time they drove up for a weekend. I had always thought our garden with the orchard trees in blossom and the view through to the fields and woods provided a lovely romantic setting. So it proved to be, for in the summer, Rodney and Vicki came to stay and Rodney asked me if he could marry Vicki. Their engagement was announced in the Telegraph.

Martin whipped in most Saturdays and Vicki and Rodney would join us when up from London for a day's hunting. Was it Jorrocks who coined the phrase, *"Happy as a beagler"*? It could surely only have been written by a hunting man? I have hunted all day, sometimes soaked to the skin and buffeted by hail and snow storms, and never felt so gloriously happy and exhilarated. At the end of the day we all returned to the house of our host on whose land we had hunted.

Kicking off our muddy boots in the porch or on the stone floor of the farmhouse, we washed our hands and waited in turn for large cups of hot steaming tea. A feast is laid before us and nothing tastes so good after a day running in the fresh air as a beagle tea. Surrounded by the happy beaglers we discuss the merits of the day's hunting with the Master and thank him for the day's sport.

Having hunted for over fifty years with the same pack of hounds, I find it only natural that many things have changed in the hunting field. When I first joined the hunt in 1934 all the lady members wore hats and tweed skirts, breeches were permissible but *never* trousers. If the meet was at a private house it was not unusual for whippers-in and followers to be offered a bath before coming down to tea where we waited for the entrance of the Master. But one thing will never change and that is the thrilling music of the hounds in full cry.

Sometimes after a day's hunting some of our friends stayed the night. A curious occurrence happened one night after we had all gone to bed. Anthony Harris was sleeping in Mother's old room at the end of the corridor. Next door the cloakroom had the original old fashioned Victorian handle which had to be pulled forward and then manually returned to its original position when flushing the loo. I had forgotten to warn Anthony about this and, lying in bed and not really asleep, I became increasingly conscious of the continual sound of water running into the large tank in the attic above my bedroom.

For some time I ignored it but eventually I got out of bed and went onto the landing where there was a gallery from which one could look down into the hall below, where I was sure I could see something glistening. I dashed back to the bedroom and put on my dressing gown, then returned and switched on the lights. Sure enough there must have been 2-3" of water lying on the parquet flooring which covered the entire ground floor of the house.

Martin happened to be out that evening so I dashed down in bare feet to the kitchen for a broom and opened the porch and outer doors of the house. Then I paddled down the long corridor to the loo and pushed the handle hard back. I started to brush as fast as I could, sweeping the water through the door and down the steps. At first it seemed to make little difference but Martin arrived and he joined me. Fortunately the door to the sitting room had been fast shut with a mat outside which had prevented water flooding the carpet. Not a single block of parquet flooring was disturbed and we never told Anthony!

When hunting finished in March, Jo and I continued to have our weekly remunerative stalls at Neston during the summer.

Vicki and Rodney were married on 31st October 1970 and went to live in Buckinghamshire. Jenny, who shared the flat with Vicki in London, was one of the bridesmaids and Martin was Best Man. They had not met before but Martin was convinced that she was the girl he wanted to marry.

I am not surprised Martin was so attracted to her. Her

golden hair, when Martin first met her, was bound round her head in the Scandinavian fashion of her country which suited her particular type of beauty. Her retrousé little nose and sparkling blue eyes added to her appeal. She was employed by the Dairy Council in London and often appeared on television. At one time she was sent to Ireland to meet Barbara Mullen who was housekeeper in Dr Finlay's Casebook, when she was promoting a film for the National Dairy Council, and she also gave advice to Vincent Price for one of his TV serials.

Like Vicki and Rodney, they also became engaged in the orchard. It was a happy occasion for all of us and has been so ever since as I have acquired a most caring daughter-in-law.

Until Martin was married, he and I continued to live in Hollinsclose. But, as I was becoming increasingly arthritic, it became obvious that I should consider moving to a smaller house, possibly in Christleton village. However, when discussing this subject one evening, the idea of converting the stable block seemed an attractive alternative especially as we already owned the building. Martin and I had fun planning the layout. He had been increasingly working as an architect with his firm for some years and was planning to start his own business as soon as possible after his marriage to Jenny.

As soon as Martin had drawn up all the plans for the conversion of the stable into a three bedroomed house and had obtained planning permission, the plans were sent out to tender. It was some time before we received replies from all the firms Martin had selected but when the estimates arrived we found the quotations were far in excess of the budget figure. The sale of Hollinsclose would cover our expenses in the end but we had no wish to be burdened with a bridging loan from the bank in the interim period nor did we want to put Hollinsclose on the market before the stable block was habitable. Faced with this dilemma, we decided the only way out was for Martin to employ the workmen and supervise the conversion himself.

He had had plenty of experience working as a civil engineer with a well known building firm ever since he had left school. He knew there was a gang of six Irish brickies employed there. They were hard-working men and these gangs often moved from firm to firm picking up work wherever it was available. Martin knew they were soon ready to move on, so he took the opportunity of showing the plans for the stable conversion to the leader and asked if they would be prepared to take on the job of extending the stable into an 'L' shaped building. They said they would be free in about three weeks time to commence digging the foundations. It was agreed they would be paid weekly.

On the morning, as arranged, the men arrived at eight o'clock and Martin went out to see them with the plans. They started work immediately cutting out the trenches for the foundations. The old building stood parallel to the house, separated from it by a large cobbled yard. It comprised a coach house, a tack room with a fireplace, and a staircase leading to the room above which stretched the whole length of the building with stabling below for two horses.

Martin decided to plan the kitchen where the tack room and first stable were situated and to insert a long window in the wall over a sink, with cupboards below, which would look onto a terrace in front of the house. Part of the second stable became the cloakroom and hall with the staircase running up against the outside wall of the original building that he now extended into an 'L' shape in order to accommodate a dining room and sitting room.

A thousand breezeblocks were ordered and these were stacked on the left-hand side of the drive. As I had never seen breezeblocks before at close quarters, I went to inspect them. Picking one up I found it seemed to have the consistency of a crumbly digestive biscuit. When Martin arrived home, I told him that one block had actually broken in half in my hand. He went at once and found the whole load to be faulty. The firm supplied us with a new load but declined to remove the others, which eventually we used for the foundation of the drive. The brickies worked very hard that week finishing the foundations and building up the outer brick wall about two feet above the foundations. On Friday they were paid as agreed.

On Monday the men did not turn up and on enquiring at his firm he was told they must have taken a week's holiday to work here before returning to Ireland.

A few days later I answered a knock at the door and saw two men standing there. One of the men was powerfully built, announced that he had heard we were in need of brickies to work on an extension. I told him to come back in the evening when Martin was at home. As we wanted to get on with the work Martin employed them and hired a cement mixer and ordered a load of bricks to be delivered.

In order to get some idea of their competence before employing them on the extension, he asked them to brick up the entrance into the coach house and all the doors into the tack room and stables on the courtyard side. He called in every day at lunchtime to inspect their progress but their work was of a poor standard and frequently needed re-doing. Still, some progress was being made. When all the courtyard side of the building had been closed, an opening had to be made in the end of the building facing the road, which would now be my new garage.

There was some attractive decorative brickwork in the apex of this wall which I was keen to preserve. The burly Irishman who was working on the wall above the kitchen gave the job to his partner. It just so happened that Martin was busy that morning and I was out shopping. Without making any attempt to shore up the brickwork in the apex, the man, standing on a ladder, started to break down the wall. Suddenly the wall collapsed flinging him off the ladder. Shocked but unhurt, he ran round to his partner who was standing on the scaffolding and told him what had happened.

About this time I returned from shopping, to be faced with the gaping hole in the wall, and all the decorative brickwork in ruins and the roof of the coach house beginning to lean over at an alarming angle. I went immediately to the phone and rang Martin. He appeared in about twenty minutes, complete with a hard hat and scaffolding poles and proceeded to assemble them to the length of about 16 feet. *"Martin,"* I implored him when I realised what he was planning to do, *"please do not go in, you will be killed if the roof falls"*. He just said nothing, and I could see that he was calculating the exact position in the roof where he should erect the scaffold pole under the beam. Terrified, nearly in tears, I begged him again not to go in. The two workmen stood well away and watched with fear in the eyes. Facing the door so he could at least have a possible escape if the roof collapsed he went in and placed the scaffold pole under a beam of the roof. The moment it was stabilised, he quickly added more poles.

All the tiles on the stable roof, excepting the coach house were perished and needed replacing. A tip-up lorry load arrived one morning and I was summoned to the front door. *"Where's the building site?"* he enquired, *"to dump this load"*. *"Well you have to stack the tiles here"*, I indicated an area on our front drive which fortunately, was very wide at the front of the house. He backed up the lorry and started to tip the whole load *"Stop,"* I shouted in alarm, *"if you tip them all out many will be broken. They should be unloaded by hand"*. He looked round for some workmen. *"I will help you,"* I said and putting on a pair of thick gloves, I helped him to unload and stack the tiles. I had to be at home when the sacks of cement were delivered to see they were stored undercover. We had covered the new foundations with plastic sheeting held down by bricks.

One Friday evening Martin returned as usual to pay the two men. He climbed the scaffolding to inspect the brick work which he found to be of such poor quality that he told the Irishman that he would have to do the job again. This remark so infuriated him that he got hold of the scaffolding and shook it as hard as he could saying, his face scarlet with rage, *"You are always criticising my work"*. Martin hung on like grim death hoping and praying that the scaffolding would not collapse and hurl him to the ground. At last the workman stopped the shaking and Martin came across to the kitchen in Hollinsclose, where I was cooking, looking so white and shaken that I asked him what had happened.

When he told me what danger he had been in and how easily he could have been thrown off the scaffolding, I took off my apron and walked round to the far side of the stable where the Irishman was still standing very red in the face. *"How dare you behave like that."* I expostulated, *"by shaking the scaffolding my son could have been killed".* *"We'll pay you for this week's work and we don't want to see either of you on site again".*

Work on the stable was now at a standstill, so Martin decided to return the cement mixer, which was on hire. However we had a bit of luck. Some friends of mine were extending their house, and their builders, on hearing of our predicament gave us a call to see if they could take on the work. They promised to begin work in about two months, just after Christmas.

Joni spent Christmas with us and Jenny came too as she and Martin had much to discuss in preparation for their wedding in May at Worthing, her home town. We went for walks in the woods behind our house, helping Joni to negotiate a deep field ditch. Once in the wood Joni spent ages cutting the stems of ivy from the base of many of the trees which were being strangled by its growth. Honeysuckle wound its way through bushes and round tree stumps already in new pale leaf. Jenny and Martin gathered a sack full of fallen wood that we dragged across the fields to the house and piled on the sitting room fire to inhale its scent.

The builders arrived as promised and set to work at once on the extension. With lorry loads of brick etc, being delivered, I had to be available on site to tell the driver where to drop the load, usually through the stable yard at the back of the house. Had I not been there I am afraid we might have returned to find bricks dumped on the drive blocking our way. A girder was put in across the garage below the brickwork which Martin had had replaced as it had been before it had collapsed. Further girders at intervals supported the roof. A new drive would eventually be constructed from the main road to this garage, cutting through our boundary wall.

To a certain extent our road still retained something of its rural character. There were still bands of grass down the pavement and we had a field next to the house and still have in 1999. Sixty-foot beech and sycamore trees and a variety of cherry, and laurel grow in the roadside shrubberies shielding the houses from the traffic and decorating the roadside in spring. Street lighting had still not been installed.

In order to be certain that the gas pipes, which were already installed in the stable block, were in good condition we asked the Gas Board to send an Inspector. Two men duly arrived in dark suits and bowler hats and, after a short inspection, assured us we had nothing to worry about. We wanted to insure against possibility of having a newly laid drive dug up on order to lay new pipes from the stable to the mains outside in the road, but 'the best laid schemes' were to prove otherwise.

As the mains water was on the other side of the road our pipes were laid beneath the drive to the gateway. The Highways Department and the County Council and the police were notified that on a certain day a trench would have to be cut across the main road 6 feet below the surface. Martin had heard of a machine called a Ditchwitch, which would cut a slot big enough to take the pipe.

On the day the machine arrived, half the road was coned off. There were at least ten traffic policemen marshalling the cars down the far side of the road much to the relief of the drivers who eyed with alarm the enormous wheel which, with a deafening screech, cut through the surface of the road scattering stone over the surface. It took two days for this machine to complete the trench.

When the workmen had laid the floor of the bedroom landing it was imperative that the roof should be built on as soon as possible. The marrying of the roof of the old building into the extension was so complicated that Martin built a scale model for the builders to refer to.

Every evening Martin and I would climb the stairs after the workmen had left to view their day's progress. They had a low bench under the window on which they kept their tools. We were standing there when we noticed a small piece of wood about 7" x 3" on which there was some writing in pencil. Curious, we picked it up and this is what it said. *"This house was built by J.W Meyers of Christleton for Mr Booth of Chester, plastering done by Johnston of Liverpool in the year 1884. Sept. 29th. J.V. Wright working in the room over the saddle room. W. Dean is laying loft floor, both of Christleton."* Written on the top edge of the wood, *"Please to take notice Joseph Meyers was the boss of this job"*. They had found the small piece of wood tucked in the old beams of the stable block.

In 1989 I had a sandstone date stone cut and inserted in the brick wall of the stable.

CHAPTER 15

The third member of my family in need of care and affection, was Joni. I tried to spend a day with him once a month. I always took our lunch, for which he was pathetically grateful as he lived mostly on tinned food, but it was the companionship he craved.

We played a card game called 'Black Jack' all afternoon. It was a perfect game for two people and we had endless fun. Poor darling, he was terribly lonely and frustrated. Nearly all his sailing friends had married and moved away so even if he did make the effort, with his gammy leg, to walk down the long flight of steps from his flat, he really had nowhere to go.

His main sorties were to one of the local yacht clubs of which he was a member where he spent the evening amongst yachting friends. He was no longer able to compete in the races and Dolphin, his Mersey Mylne, was laid up. He never complained about his inability to sail any longer but drowned his sorrows in endless glasses of whisky. Most of his friends understood his situation and were very sorry for him.

On the rare occasions that he became so inebriated that he was reduced to tears, they brought him home and rang me up. As it was often 11 o'clock at night, Martin came over with me and we did what we could to comfort him. I returned early the following morning to see how he was, expecting to find him sleeping, but to my astonishment he answered the door bell, fully dressed and trying to make every effort to appear as normal as possible. He looked ghastly. His skin was the colour of green putty and was shining with sweat. I didn't need to ask how he felt.

We went into his siting room and I made some coffee. *"Joni,"* I said, *"why don't you come and live in Chester? You could have a flat looking onto the river and we could see a lot more off each other"*. But he was not to be persuaded. He loved his flat with the view to the Welsh hills and the shipping on the Mersey and he could potter down to see Dolphin in the yard at Rock Ferry.

I was horrified to see he had sold the three valuable oil paintings which Mother had given him from Dad's study. He would have had no idea of their value and probably sold them for a song.

I was so concerned about his condition that I made an appointment with his doctor, who more or less, told me, in no uncertain terms, that he had washed his hands of him. Joni had been to see him as he was getting a lot of pain in his straight leg and he had told him that the only way to improve the circulation in his leg was to give up smoking. Joni had not followed his advice.

I could not help feeling angry with the doctor who appeared to have no sympathy for a war casualty and I more or less told him so. He then agreed he would arrange for him to be admitted to Clatterbridge Hospital where the circulation in his leg would be investigated.

I visited him two or three times and found him very unhappy as he was deprived of whisky and cigarettes. He longed to get back to his flat but there had been no mention of his discharge. Then fate played into his hands.

The front door of his flat had been seen to have been left open by a policeman on patrol late at night. On finding the flat empty, he made enquiries amongst the neighbours the following day who told him where Joni could be found. He visited the hospital and asked if he was fit enough to return to see if anything had been stolen. Joni was now a walking patient and he leapt at the opportunity of vowing that once out he would not return. He cadged a lift home in the police car!

Martin rang me from the office one day to tell me the electricians would be arriving that day and would I tell them where I wanted the sockets and switches fitting. These decisions are extremely difficult, as at that time I did not know exactly where my furniture would fit and what and where I would need power points in the kitchen and the rest of the house. My only stipulation that all sockets were to be fitted about 3 foot above floor level.

We never had central heating fitted in Hollinsclose as it would have been enormously costly but we were not used to it anyway as we had never felt the need of it as children in The Hollies. With coal and gas fires in the rooms we had always been comfortably warm and so it had been at Kilmorey. However, as we were converting the stable, Martin decided it was now necessary to install central heating, thus eliminating the fitting of fireplaces or gas fires in the bedrooms.

When all the work had been completed the gas was turned on, but nothing happened. The workman went into the garage to inspect the pipe which brought the gas in from the mains and found it to be like lace. I was furious and told him how we had had it inspected by men from the Gas Board who assured us it was in working order as we did not want the new drive to be disturbed. The only way now was to cut a trench in the border on our side of the new fence. I watched with a sickening heart the great mounds of pure yellow clay piled up on each side of the trench before the gas main was laid.

When the trench was refilled most of the top soil had vanished and though, over the many years we have lived here, peat and leaf mould has been copiously applied to the area I don't think the border has ever recovered.

I had been working on my watercolours and decided to have an exhibition before Christmas. An acquaintance of Martin's had a restaurant in St. Werburgh Street, Chester. As he had a lot of vacant wall space, I asked him if I could display my paintings there. He agreed at once, saying he would get one of the waiters to help Martin to hang them, as this is a painstaking and tedious job because the frames were not all the same size.

It was a lovely place for me to have an exhibition as I could sit in the comfort at one of the tables all day. They received a good deal of interest and it was heart warming and encouraging for me to hear so many flattering remarks. I sold very well and acquired quite a few commissions. The following year I repeated the exhibition.

In between exhibitions I kept them on display in a dentist's waiting room, in an art shop and in the Nuffield Nursing Home, keeping my name in public view.

One day, walking down Bridge Street, I noticed that

one of the Building Societies had a large, almost empty window. The glass of which came down to a wide windowsill about 2 foot from the ground. What a perfect place for an exhibition, I thought, as I had plenty of easels to stand at the back and I could display eight watercolours on the cill. I went in at once and asked if I could speak to the Manager, promising I would bring some samples of my work for him to approve before making a decision.

This was a much more commercial proposition than the restaurant as once I had set up my display, I had no need to be there. Added to which almost every passer-by stopped to have a look. The Manager was quite agreeable and I placed a card in the foreground with my name and telephone number. I also gave the staff permission to pass on enquiries to me and receive cheques.

I had about eighteen paintings on show and sold about fourteen of them during the week. I noticed that all the paintings depicting a fisherman sold very quickly and I was thrilled with the result and repeated the exhibition the following year.

The builders had promised we would be able to move in before Christmas. It was my job to choose the fireplaces, bathroom and kitchen fittings and I was very lucky over the last two items. Driving along the road towards Upton, I passed a firm who supplied bathroom and kitchen fittings. There was a notice on the window saying, "Closing Down Sale. Everything Half Price". I stopped and went in at once.

They had quite a few displays on show and I had no difficulty choosing everything for the bathroom and a complete kitchen layout with cupboards, sink and wall fittings. I could hardly believe my luck that they really were half price, but was reassured when the Manager showed me the catalogue with all the original prices.

During this time, too, I had to be available at Hollinsclose to show people round the house and to arrange for a firm to erect a fence between the two houses, cutting the garden in half. We decided on a ranch fence which we thought would blend in with the shrubs.

As the stable building now looked into the orchard we decided to call the new conversion Orchard House. In a way I was inheriting the best half of our old garden. We would miss the swimming pool, which Martin had built, but we had the orchard which was now under-planted with many daffodils and drifts of snowdrops. We also had the pond and the view across the field to the woods.

One day the front door bell rang and standing on the steps was a charming young mother with her two children. I had decided that I would like to have a young family in our old house and I had to chose carefully as they would be our neighbours.

That evening I met her husband and after they had had a look around the property they decided to meet the asking price and would like to move in about one month later. We reckoned, with a bit of luck, that Orchard House would be ready for me to move in then. Martin and Jenny were now married and were moving into a little town house just down the road.

Now I had to sort out what furniture I could accommodate in a much smaller house. All the remaining furniture, pictures, china etc, that had belonged to Mother and had not been claimed by any of my sisters had to be

Martin and Jenny were now married and were moving into a little town house just down the road.

sorted and packed up to go to the sale rooms, the more ordinary articles to a local sale room and antique pieces were sent to Sothebys in Chester. The fact that I had been handling antiques for many years now stood me in good stead because I was able to insist that the pieces were catalogued properly.

The dear old Donegal carpet had to be cut down again to fit the smaller dining room but its glorious colours, now slightly faded, but still unworn, continued to complement the oak of the dining room furniture. For the sitting room I chose a pale duck egg blue carpet. All the other carpets were cut down to fit the smaller bedrooms. The curtains, with slight adjustments, all fitted the new house.

As the new drive cut through the rose beds on the

front lawn and the soil was rose-sick, I decided to forego them and replace them with turf. The wide border which had been on the south side of the stable, where I had grown delphiniums, had been replaced by a courtyard in front of the new house. As there is a considerable drop in the land level on the side of the stable, we built a retaining wall the length of the courtyard with a flight of steps down to the lower lawn. All the borders and pathways were eventually replaced in order to balance the new building. This work I enjoyed doing with the occasional help of an old gardener. My new neighbours had settled in our old house and I became very fond of their children.

I had always grown a lot of vegetables in a long wide border the length of the garden. I grew peas, runner beans, sprouting broccoli, onions, leeks, radishes and lettuce. The latter had to be protected with netting against the pigeons and rabbits. I had a lot of squirrels too, but they did not seem to touch the vegetables.

With plenty to occupy me, I soon got used to my new home which Martin had designed so attractively. The rooms were spacious and full of light from the bay windows. It had a cottagy atmosphere with the chintz covered furniture and beamed ceiling. I had arranged to have a slate mantelpiece and surround installed in the sitting room to remind me of the slate quarries in Pennant Valley. A heavy brass Victorian fender stood on the hearth.

I asked Joni to come and stay frequently in the summer. Like me, and all our family, he was a keen gardener and he helped me a lot, tying up the runner beans and staking the peas. He spent hours picking off caterpillars, collecting snails and making bonfires. We waged war against ground elder and thistles which encroached from the fields and we laughed and were happy together doing the things we loved best.

When planning the layout of the rooms in Orchard House, Martin had incorporated a small room between the bedrooms where I could keep my antiques on display and pack them up for fairs or car boot sales. In my travels I had acquired a knowledge of specialist dealers and was often able to supply them with the wares they collected, negotiating a reasonable profit for myself. This was a much more satisfactory way for me to sell than through any of the auction houses, as the money for the sale was paid to me there and then.

Joni and I sometimes went antique hunting together as he was as keen as I to find a bargain. When he had worked as an estate agent he quite frequently came across abandoned articles in empty houses. Brass and copper coal scuttles, black with age and coal dust, and damaged oil paintings were the most common finds in cellars, garages or old barns where they had been thrown in a corner, discarded by their owners as worthless, or for which they had no further use. But was it not always so, and are we little different today?

In a derelict garage beneath a pile of leaves my brother found a large 18th century oil painting of a dish of fish with rod, net and a creel which he brought to me to restore. Now cleaned and varnished, it hangs in the hall to be much enjoyed by the fishing members of the family. In an empty house on the Yorkshire moors, we found in the larder some Bristol blue cut glass globes set in a purpose built wooden carrying tray with handles. They were filled with liquid. When we returned home I called at the Museum in Chester and upon giving a description of the bottles, was told they were Victorian fire extinguishers. They were very decorative, but we left them there.

After a country house sale I noticed, left on the table used by the auctioneers, a large white square dish with attractive twisted handles decorated with worn gold leaf, which they had been using as an ashtray. Underneath was the Royal Worcester mark.

Holding up the sagging ceiling of an empty cottage in Yorkshire I spotted a beautifully carved mahogany pole suitable for use as a lamp standard. It must have, at one time, helped to support the canopy of a four poster bed and was probably one of a pair.

Books are frequently abandoned. In the bedroom of an old vicarage in a Welsh valley we found hundreds of books lying on the floor, all written in Welsh, naturally! In that same vicarage on the mantelpiece I found, left by previous owner, no doubt, a bottle of medicine beside which lay a solid silver teaspoon, the bowl black from the last dose from the bottle - a perfect vital clue for an Agatha Christie thriller?

In the loft of a derelict farm we found an old cabinet, the wood grey with age, damp and cobwebs. Inside, the drawers were full of hundreds of birds eggs.

Whilst exploring the kitchen of an ancient empty farmhouse I spotted a built-in corner cupboard. As I opened the door, a cascade of large oval Staffordshire strainers from vegetable tureens cascaded onto the floor at my feet. The two that didn't break, decorated in blue with classical scenery now hang on my kitchen wall.

When we packed up the contents of my Mother's home, I found, on the dressing table in the housemaid's bedroom, a beautiful oval Spode dish decorated with full blown roses, which Mother had placed there to contain her brush and comb. Now it is displayed in a china cabinet.

As children we often had tea in the garden by the tennis court during the summer when we returned from school. As the china teasets were too good for garden tea, Mother bought a quantity of cheap and cheerful Clarisse Cliff pottery which was more suitable. When we divided all the tea and dinner services between us, nobody wanted the Clarisse Cliff pottery so it was all abandoned; like our ancestors before us, we had no further use for it.

Friends of ours who lived at Tranmere Old Hall, faced with more furniture than they could accommodate in their new smaller house, removed all the button-backed bucket-shaped Victorian armchairs into the stable yard and set fire to them. At one time John's father offered us some very large armchairs which were covered in crimson silk velvet. I am afraid we thought they were very old fashioned and as we had not room for them in our small Victorian house, declined the offer.

Some time after we were married, we took the children into Wales for a walk. I wanted to see if the primroses were in flower on the two long drives which gave access to the Elizabethan Nerquis Hall near Mold.

For quite a long time the Hall appeared to be empty as the great walled garden was overgrown and the greenhouses along the walls collapsed and derelict. John walked ahead and then came back saying, "*I think the Hall is empty*". Clutching my bunch of flowers, I followed him to the front door which we found to be wide open. We went into the large entrance hall and called out, whereupon the owner, Mr Tringham, appeared and invited us to come in.

We followed him into his panelled study at the back of the house where he was sorting out some furniture, picture frames etc and told us he was selling up and leaving the house. He appeared to be rather sad and lonely and he reminded me of my brother.

We stayed chatting with him when he suddenly remarked, "*Would you like some books? I have had a firm up from London to see them and they have offered me one penny for each volume so I am going to burn the lot, you can help yourself.*"

We followed him upstairs to the little oval shaped library full of excited anticipation. The shelves were stocked with hundreds of small leather bound 18th century books, the leather now bleached to the palest cream and brittle dry. We slipped a few out of the shelves, they were all printed in French. We took half a dozen English Books with such titles as, "Letters to my Son in Prison" simply as a memento of the occasion. Twenty years later the antique dealers were selling leather bound books by the yard.

Everything goes full circle. The things that we despised fifty years ago we would now be more than happy to possess. We let them slip through our fingers and it took the Antiques Road Show to bring us to our senses.

CHAPTER 16

A Law School had been established in Christleton and the students were searching for accommodation which was at a premium. My next door neighbours in Hollinsclose decided to take some students and suggested I did also as I had two empty bedrooms. At first I resisted but eventually decided to try it as both Martin and Vicki were married and living away from home.

I tentatively booked in two young men who had called at the house. It was a tremendous success. Not only was it a great help financially but my home felt like a family home again. Over the following years I had many young men and women and became so very fond of them in turn that when they left it felt like losing one of the family.

Two of the boys I had staying with me were interested in historical buildings so at weekends I took them to see Beeston, Ruthin and Denbigh castles. I also took them 'sticking'.

Introduced to 'sticking' when I was a child in Grassington when we went to the woods with Mrs Birch, I continued to be a 'sticker' all my life. Joni and I collected boot loads full from Wales and now I took my students. Having lived in the heart of Manchester and never having the need of such an occupation, they loved to accompany me on summer evenings to a wood nearby. This was a very old neglected wood and everywhere were fallen branches about the thickness of your arm. I told them to throw them out of the wood onto the lane where they broke into pieces and I collected them and packed them into the boot of the car. Thus laden we turned for home to enjoy the fruits of our labours.

We unloaded the wood into the shed and, carrying a basket full of logs to the sitting room, I felt as if I were bringing the country into the house. I lit the fire, placing some ivy covered logs on top of the coal; the splintered bark showed pale shreds of pith which crackled in the blaze, and the scent poured into the room like all the woods you have ever walked in, full of damp leaf mould.

My father, in his way, also loved the scent of burning wood. Every year he had a load of silver birch logs delivered to our house in Oxton which was poured through a hatch into the cellar. When the sitting room fire was lit he would peel off a piece of bark from a birch log with the fire tongs, light it and hold it over the hearth where it twisted and turned, pervading the room with its sweet pungent scent.

One day, when I was shopping in Chester, I suddenly felt as if I had been hit in the eye, by a bluebottle. The following day, feeling there was something wrong, I made an appointment to see my doctor who sent me at once to the Royal Infirmary where I was seen by an eye specialist. After a careful examination he told me I had a detached retina. "*What does that mean,*" I enquired fearfully. "*It means immediate ward,*" he replied. I asked if I could ring Martin and he arrived about half an hour later with a bunch of red roses. I was taken to the ward in a wheelchair while they prepared a bed in the Eye Ward. I was stunned.

A water bed was prepared for me and I was told that I

would have to lie still on my right side. At first I was distracted by the sound of the motor running beneath the pillow but soon got used to it. My eye was operated on the following day. The first thing I remember was the surgeon encouraging me to try and take big breaths. I suppose I must have tried, but remember only the ghastly struggles to breathe at all. *"The cardiac arrest hasn't helped,"* I heard someone saying. Sometime later I realised I was now in bed with a nurse sitting by me encouraging me all the time, but I felt as though I was drowning with no air in my lungs, only a deadly, stifling pain.

After two weeks the eye specialist decided it was time to remove the bandage from my eyes. At last I thought I was going to see again, at least from my good eye. But when the dressings were removed I was totally blind. The disappointment was catastrophic. Weak from lying all day in one position, I think I cried uncontrollably. Had the nurse just said, *"You may not see clearly at first because your good eye has to adjust,"* I would not have worried.

However, as I was now allowed to get up each day, my priority was to get strong so that I could come home. Feeling along the length of my bed and turning left, holding the end of the bed, I reckoned I would soon get to the end of the next bed and so on down the ward. Patients watching my progress were very helpful, telling me when I had reached the end of the ward or if there was anything in my way. I stuck at this day after day getting a little stronger but still not able to see. When I reached the end of the ward where there was a row of windows above the radiator I used to feel the glass with an agony of longing to see out.

When I was ready to be discharged I had to wear pinhole glasses which were all blacked out except for a tiny pinhole of light. I was beginning to see a little. After about a month I had to wear dark sunglasses for three months. I was told I must not lift any weights or garden or bend my head down or drive my car for at least six months. I was still pretty weak as I could not walk about, being only able to see about three yards ahead. My students were very kind often bringing me cups of tea and spending a little of their time to have a chat. Gradually my sight returned. All this of course meant no trips to Runcorn or stalls at Neston.

Martin and Jenny who had been to see me every evening in hospital and paid many visits to see me when I got home, decided to have a dinner party just before Christmas. As it was not safe yet for me to travel by car we had decided to have Christmas at my house when Vicki and Rodney could stay with me and we could all be together.

At about 7 o'clock I got up off my chair to go to bed. Almost at once I was conscious of a black substance pouring down in my eye. I guessed it was blood. Terrified, I went from chair to chair wringing my hands, not knowing what to do. At last I decided to ring my doctor at his home, which you were able to do then, if surgery was over. He answered at once and I told him what had happened and begged him to come and see me. *"Oh"*, he said, *"I wouldn't worry if I were you, I'd go to bed"*. Half an hour later, I decided to ring the eye specialist who had performed the operation, and seek his advice. His wife answered the phone and spoke to her husband who advised me to ring for an ambulance to the Infirmary where the specialist on duty would see me.

I knew I couldn't go without letting Martin know, so, reluctantly, I rang his home. He said he would come at once and collect me. After about an hour's wait at Casualty in the

Infirmary as it was Christmas Eve, the doctor saw me and said that I would have to be admitted to the ward. Dreadfully unhappy and unable to sleep I was thankful to see the Specialist who came at about 6 o'clock on Christmas morning to look at my eye. He told me that my eye was in an awful mess and implied that nothing could be done then. *"Well, can I go home?"* I pleaded, *"My daughter and her husband and my brother will be there"*. I think he knew the eye was past repairing and he said, *"Under the circumstances there is little I can do so, yes, you can go home."*

During the time I had been in hospital I had heard of Mr Grey, a well known eye specialist in Liverpool, so after Christmas I asked my doctor if I could consult him. After an appointment was made I was taken by ambulance to St Paul's Eye Hospital where, after a week's rest and many hours spent with his consultant, the day came for his visit. The patients in the ward were asked to move into the day room and Sister conducted Mr Grey to my bedside and, after introducing him, left us together.

Mr Grey sat down on a chair by my bed and said kindly, *"I am afraid the retina is full of holes, it is like lace. I could repair it for you, but it is very fragile and may not hold"*. I felt I could not go through it all again so I said, *"I think I will let it go as I have one good eye"*. He nodded understandingly and soon left. Martin arrived at about 7 o'clock as he had done every evening. I was dressed and ready to go home with him.

No one who has not experienced blindness can imagine what it was like to see again. As we drove away into the Cheshire countryside on our way home, the joy of release from months in hospital and the sight of the fields, trees and sky is impossible to describe. I did not talk much, nor could I, as tears of happiness were choking me. I am sure Martin knew just how I felt, driving slowly, so that I could regain confidence and know it was not just a dream that I really could see the grass at the side of the road.

The first thing I knew I must do on returning home was to build up my strength and morale which had been severely undermined. During my monthly visits to the Infirmary for a check-up I had been told categorically that, *"Having one detached retina, I was sure to have the other"*. Somehow, if I was to live as normal a life as possible, I had to fight this fear and come to terms with reality. I was blind in one eye. My surgeon had also told me that I was at risk going in a car for fear of an accident as any violent jerk could detach the other retina. *"If I drove the car myself I would be safer?"* I enquired. *"Well, yes"*, he reluctantly agreed. *"That would be safer because holding the steering wheel will save you from being thrown about"*. Making a mental note of that remark I was determined to drive again as soon as possible.

Almost to the day that the 6 months were up Martin came with me whilst I drove round the local lanes. As soon as I was able to drive I couldn't wait to get back to my stall at Neston. The Beagle season was over and Jo readily offered to carry in boxes of china from the car to my stall; without her help I could not have taken the risk. There were always willing hands to put my stall up and their kindness helped in my recovery. The more I occupied my day the less time I had to worry about my eye. My friends soon booked me up for bridge and I was able to get to Runcorn and other antique hunting grounds. Sadly, I had to give up gardening but I could paint and write. I had had such a welcome, too, from my student who had looked after my house so well while I was in hospital.

Joni came over to stay frequently. He was a great comfort to me, just by his presence, though his appearance was now very fragile. We had need of each other and were at ease in one another's company. Because of his heart condition he had to go for short walks every day. I never let him go across the field by himself, though my arthritic hip was becoming very painful but he couldn't walk far with his bad leg as the circulation had not improved.

Sometime after John died I had joined the National Association of Decorative and Fine Arts Society (NADFAS) with some friends. I had always enjoyed listening to good lectures which were on a variety of subjects and it was a day out as we occasionally had a pub lunch beforehand.

The husband of one of my friends was Chapter Clerk to Chester Cathedral. He was approached by the Dean and asked if he could suggest any members of NADFAS who would be willing to restore and document all the books in the Cathedral library. I had the honour of being asked and leapt at the opportunity. We had two full days training by a professional restorer and four of us commenced work, one day a week, in the spring. The work, of course, was voluntary.

To begin with we approached the work with some trepidation, knowing how easy it was to damage leather by using the wrong dressing. We had came to terms with the mysteries of Kluzel G and the responsibility of improving the bindings, cleaning and repairing the pages and cataloguing the books. We gained enormous satisfaction and looked forward every week to our visits to the Cathedral library where we worked for about four hours, each day for a period of three years.

I found researching at the Record Office very therapeutic. I had to shut out all the worries and really concentrate on finding information from the thousands of books on Cheshire that covered the shelves around the room. There were also card indexes for reference.

The fields at the bottom of our garden were very old meadows. The ridge and furrow marking could clearly be seen when the rays of the setting sun slanted across them. When we first came to live in Hollinsclose I often collected mushrooms on these fields and blackberries from the hedge bordering the ditch which fed our pond. In one of these fields is a large marl pit. I had always been given to understand that marl was another name for clay, even in the dictionary it is described as soil composed of a mixture of lime and clay used as a fertilizer. As the soil in this area of Littleton is very heavy clay the habit of using marl to spread over the already clay soil didn't seem to make sense to me. So off I went to the Records Office to really find out and this led to the article I wrote which was published in Cheshire Life.

I had been working on one of my articles when my phone rang. A friend of Joni's rang to tell me that Joni had inadvertently burnt his feet and had been taken to Clatterbridge Hospital. *"How on earth did he do that?"* I enquired, horrified at the news. Peter told me that as far as he had been able to question Joni, he had got into his bath with the geyser, which supplied the hot water, still running. He must have had some sort of blackout as he had no idea how long he was in the bath. Fortunately, when he returned to the sitting room, Peter noticed he was in a state of shock but it wasn't until he sat down that he noticed his feet and ankles. He immediately rang for an ambulance and accompanied him to Clatterbridge Hospital.

He was kept in for one night after his feet were dressed and returned home the following day, when the ambulance men had to carry him from the road and up the long flight of steps to his flat. They had not enquired if there was anyone to look after him but said they would return the next day to take him back for the dressings to be replaced. I cannot think why they had not kept him in hospital as he was quite incapable of walking anywhere even to get a glass of water and he was in a lot of pain. I drove over to see him and we discussed how we could get him to Chester as it was only five days to Christmas.

He was collected by ambulance each day to have his feet dressed, an incredibly painful procedure, so I arranged to meet him at the Hospital where he was pushed in a wheelchair to my car. The hospital had supplied some thick socks over his dressings and on these he managed to hobble across the courtyard and into my sitting room where he collapsed, thankfully, onto my couch.

Martin and Jenny now had three small children. They all came over to see him and cheer him up as they adored their Uncle Joni. He slept on the couch and had all his meals there and each day I took him to the Infirmary for dressings. Somehow he kept up a brave face and on Christmas Day joined us for lunch. With a supreme effort he pulled crackers and laughed with the grand-children wearing a paper hat as a sign of his courage.

In the early evening he had to go to the cloakroom which was at the end of the entrance hall. On the way back he collapsed. I ran to him. *"Joni are you alright?"* *"No"*, he said, *"I cannot stand up."* As he was a dead weight I knew I couldn't help him, so I called the Infirmary and asked for an ambulance. The porter replied that they had no ambulances and could I bring him in by car. I told him that I was unable to lift him off the floor as I had had a detached retina. *"Well sorry luv,"* he replied. I argued, *"Can't you think of anything?"* *"Well"* he replied, *"you might try the police"*.

To my relief the police promised to call. They arrived about an hour later with a wheelchair but were not too pleased to be called out.

After he arrived at the hospital I spoke to a ward sister and asked her if I had done the right thing. *"Definitely"*, she replied, *"he should never have been allowed out of hospital with his feet in that condition"*. I called on him later that evening and found half the hospital in darkness. *"We always try to close down most of the wards over Christmas"*, one of the nurses told me. I found the long dark corridors very eerie and on mentioning it when I got home, Sophie, Martin's eldest daughter aged 8, immediately offered to accompany me. *"I'll come with you Granny,"* she said. *"I'd like to."*

So over the Christmas period I was grateful to feel that little hand in mine as we groped our way through the dimly lit hospital to the ward.

CHAPTER 17

Joni was now back home and being cared for by his home help. So I had no need to go over so often and climb up the long flight of stairs to his flat, a journey which was becoming increasingly difficult and painful for me. By late spring he was driving again and decided to take me to Llangernyw. There was a little antique shop in the village and he knew I wanted to collect half a dozen pairs of hanging shelves. They were made by local craftsmen and were much in demand as people became increasingly interested in collecting small pieces of china which, they wished to display. For me they were good money spinners, as I doubled my outlay.

Driving home one day from Chester I pulled up at a Belisha crossing to allow a man with his two children to walk across. As soon as they had reached the side of the road, I released my brake and was just engaging my gears, when I was hit in the back of the car and sent flying up the road. The driver of the car that had hit me pulled up beside me and got out. Flustered and full of apologies, he admitted that he had not been concentrating, *"Well, thank God"* I said, *"that you didn't hit me when the children were on the crossing"*. We exchanged names and addresses and insurance companies, etc, before I drove home to assess the damage. The back of the bumper was driven in and the lid of the boot had been forced and was flapping about as the lock had been broken. As it happened, my car had been booked in to have a new gearbox fitted as I could only use two gears, 1st and top.

I had only been in the house a couple of hours, when I had a desperately worried phone call from my son-in-law, Rod, Vicki had been rushed to hospital with an ectopic pregnancy and there was no-one to look after their three year old daughter, Wendy. Rod and Vicki lived in Marsworth in Buckinghamshire. I said I would come immediately, completely forgetting in my anxiety about the state of my car and that I was suffering slightly from whiplash.

I packed a few things in a suitcase and drove to my local garage, having tied up the flapping boot with some rope. *"Can you please look at the back wheels and the chassis as I have to drive to Bucks"*. *"Not in that car"* he said. *"Yes"* I replied, *"I must go. I have only one hill to climb to Tarvin where I turn right to Tarporley and after that I can pretty well keep in top gear when I get on the motorway."* He put the car up on the ramp and had a look round. *"The chassis is alright"* he said, *"and the wheels, but you'll have some problems with your gears"*. He shook his head knowing that he could not stop me. I filled the car up with petrol, crashed into gear and drove out of the garage, not wanting to wait another minute.

Somehow I forced the car up the Tarvin Road to the turn to Tarporley and was then on the straight to the M6 south. My biggest problem was driving through any built-up area as I had to depend on my brakes to slow the car down. Once I came off the motorway driving was much more difficult, as there were no traffic lights then, only roundabouts at busy junctions, which I had to negotiate in bottom gear. I arrived late in the afternoon, desperately anxious about Vicki. Rod was horrified when he saw my car and offered me the use of Vicki's car whilst I was staying there and said he would get some repairs done on the lock of my boot before I had to drive home.

Vicki had a transfusion of five pints of blood and was in intensive care. I swept up my darling little grand daughter and hugged her tight against me, burying my face in her mop of curls. The softness of her little body and her kisses comforted me a great deal. That night Rod and I sat up playing backgammon into the early hours of the morning when we heard she was out of danger. Two years later Vicki had a son, Roly.

Back home I continued to garden, see my friends and collect antiques. I also played quite a lot of bridge which I enjoyed enormously. When the weather was fine during the summer I often took a picnic lunch and drove into the Cheshire or Wirral countryside looking for suitable subjects to start a watercolour which I could finish at home. I also went on a sketching holiday to Yorkshire with a friend. At the end of July I joined Martin and Jenny at Abersoch where they rented, every year, a house on the headland near the yacht club. It is a glorious position, an absolute sun trap looking across the bay to Harlech Castle. I painted a great deal there too, and learned to fly a kite which I used as a subject when painting children on the beach.

The vegetable patch, which I had cultivated the whole length of the garden, was becoming too much for me. Although it gave me immense pleasure picking my own peas and beans and growing onions, salad and sprouting broccoli, I was unable to dig any more or to prepare the soil properly. At about the same time Martin's young family were outgrowing their small town house and they had to make a move.

I started looking at property in Christleton village. It is a very pretty village and has a large pond with nesting swans and many varieties of water fowl. Martin became alarmed at my suggestion of selling Orchard House. It would suit his family perfectly, possessing a large garden with uninterrupted views to the fields and woods at the back of the house where the children could run and play in safety. He drafted some plans suggesting how he could built on a new wing providing me with adequate accommodation and the privacy of my own front door.

At first I was not too keen on the idea of leaving my lovely home, and the loss and companionship of my law students, but the more I thought about it, I could see there were many advantages. With the sale of Martin and Jenny's house, he would have the capital to build the extension. An unexpected bonus also helped his finances. Martin and Vicki inherited a country house in Brecon, the property of their Uncle Jim, who was John's youngest brother.

Martin and I poured over the plans for the extension. He was master at fitting everything I would need into a smaller space. In Orchard House, too, alterations would have to be made so that the three children could have their own bedrooms. My bedroom was a very large room with windows at both ends and Martin planned to divide this room in half. The house would then have four bedrooms.

Whilst we were occupied with the alterations to the two houses my hip was becoming increasingly painful where it joined the damaged sacroiliac joint. Because I had had a cardiac arrest with my last operation on my eye, I vowed I would never go through that ordeal again but I was walking with such difficulty now that I thought it was not fair to the family if something could be done and I plucked up courage and visited my doctor who suggested I saw Doctor Campbell at the Nuffield. I had a lot of tests and consultation with the anaesthetist.

I was naturally very nervous knowing the danger I had to face but Mr Campbell assured me that I would have the operation at the Countess where I could be near the intensive care unit if anything went wrong. On the morning of the operation Vicki sat with me playing Scrabble till I was due to go to theatre. It was hard going but she never left my side, refusing to go for a coffee. Fortunately, all went well though the anaesthetist told me afterwards he was more than relieved at the successful outcome.

Whilst I was in hospital Martin's builders set to work with the foundation of the extension, so I returned to workmen and the incessant sound of the cement mixer. I left hospital on January 6th and it was bitterly cold, but every day, as part of my recovery, I had to walk to strengthen the muscles in my hip. It took me quite a while to get as far as our gate, but bit by bit, encouraged by the workmen I managed to walk with two sticks, to the next gate and so on down our road.

Inside, the house the extension looked tiny, the heavy grey breeze block walls adding to the feeling of claustrophobia. I had decided to have the kitchen at the front of the house facing south and my quite large sitting room facing north overlooking the garden and orchard at the rear. This is the quiet side of the house away from the sound of the traffic. I could sit here watching the cattle come into the fields and observe the many birds flying amongst the branches of the fruit trees. In spring time there was the fruit blossom and the daffodils and snowdrops I had planted in the orchard. Even my tiny bedroom in the front of the house, a third the size of the last one, felt like a little nest, as it was full of sun. I had a view of the beech trees and the rookery and the wood on the far side of the road. I had a good sized kitchen, well fitted with cupboards all round and a cloakroom but no dining room. Upstairs, besides my bedroom, there was a twin bedded spare room, bathroom and airing cupboard and a space over the front door for my desk and book shelves. I decided to call the extension Orchard Cottage.

What I had not catered for when I decided to plan the sitting room on the North side, was the lack of light and sun in the room. It was impossible for me to paint and after a year I felt depressed and frustrated. Realising that the answer was to build on a conservatory on the back of the house, I invited some local firm to come to the house. They were very helpful but the cost was too high. There was nothing for it; I would have to raise the money by painting watercolours. The subjects I chose were local views, wild flowers in their natural habitat, fishermen on the Dee and scenes in Wharfedale.

If we took down all the oil paintings in the sitting room, and set up spot lights with my various sized easels, I reckoned I could show about sixteen paintings. I would have to work very hard and planned to have two exhibitions. It took me two years to raise the extra money during which time I must have sold about twenty-five watercolours.

CHAPTER 18

The conservatory was more than a success, with glass roof and sides I have much better vision. I feel as though I am sitting in my garden, which, in a way, I am. Double doors lead to a flight of steps down to the orchard and on the shelves I have pots of geraniums. I have my breakfast there in the summer and most of the year use it as my sitting room. It is a lovely peaceful room in which I can entertain my friends and watch the rabbits and squirrels and identify the birds which flock to the feeders.

Joni was having a lot of pain in his foot. The circulation was very poor in the leg which had had the knee removed. When I could get to Wallasey to see him he was nearly always sitting with his foot raised on a stool. The District Nurse was visiting him once a week. He was always so glad to see me, a feeling that was mutual. Sometimes I used to take him out into Wales in the car but as time went on he had to keep his foot elevated to relieve the pain and finally he was admitted to hospital. I missed him very much and our excursions into Wales together.

When I visited him in hospital he looked like an animal trapped in a cage fighting to get out. I could see from the expression in his eyes the mental torture he was going through. Joni had always been a free spirit and, like me, life to him was the open air, surrounded by green fields, woods and streams and the sound of the sea. A few days later when I saw him, the nurse had put him in a wheelchair by the open window. It was a sunny day and the sunlight was on the roof tops of the houses in Wallasey where he had his flat.

When I spoke to a nurse she said they hoped to operate on his foot. She told me he had gangrene and I wondered if they were contemplating an amputation. They didn't say. The following day I found he had been put in a side ward. He was very distressed, banging his head up and down onto his knees. He begged and implored me to take him home. I will never forget the expression in his eyes, although he was heavily sedated.

"Why were they not operating?" I asked, but the nurses evaded my question and did not answer. In the end I got up at 8 in the morning and drove over to Wallasey to the hospital determined, at all costs, to speak to Sister who never seemed to be available when I visited. When I got to the hospital I went immediately to the ward and requested an interview with Sister. I was taken to her room where I asked her for a straight answer. *"Why has my brother not had his operation? He has been in hospital for three weeks"*. *"We have no anaesthetist at present,"* she replied. Did she really expect me to believe that? *"I am his sister,"* I replied, *"and I think I have a right to know what you can do for him"*. She did not answer my question and took me out into the ward.

I went over every day after that hoping perhaps I could see the specialist but they had removed Joni to a private ward. He was in a lot of pain and semi-conscious but he knew I was there. I slipped into the side of his bed and cradled his head in my arms, putting my cheek by his and living him as much as I could. *"I love you Joanie"*, he whispered. *"And I love you too Joni,"* I said. At times he appeared to be in such pain that I went out and found a

Joni had always enjoyed the sea and sailing

nurse pleading with her to give him some more morphine, but she assured me he was sedated enough, but they would come in and move him to make him easier. The following day when I visited him he was unconscious and did not know me.

I returned in the afternoon and sat by his bed till about 4.30, asking the nurse to promise to ring if his condition deteriorated. At about 8.30 that night the nurse or Sister on the ward rang Martin to let him know that Joni had little time to live. Martin told the Sister he felt I had had enough and he decided not to tell me. Early the following morning he came over to Orchard Cottage.

Later I went down the garden to the pond and lent against the trunk of the willow tree unable to cope with the gut-tearing pain of loss. I was hardly aware at first of the little steps of the children on the grass behind me. First James, so little that he could only hug me round the waist, then the arms of Lindsay and Sophie wrapped around me with their faces pressed to mine.

I rang Nora, Pye and Min and then his life-long friend, Mike Webster, who promised to come up from the south of England to give the address at the funeral, for which I was very grateful. He also promised to contact all Joni's old sailing friends. We decided he should be buried with Mum and Dad at Landican Cemetery. I covered his coffin with red roses.

Poor Mike, he was unable to finish his address but this is the gist of it. *"I was not around when John Justin Baleroy Ivory was born in 1917. He was educated at Uppingham School, from whence he proceeded into the surveying profession in Liverpool. During the late 1930's he was an active member of the Climbers Club, Oxton Hockey Club and the West Cheshire Sailing Club.*

During the war period he attained the rank of Captain with a field battalion of artillery in which he specialised in 25 pounders. Alas, in August 1942, in that far off country Iraq, he was badly wounded and a two day journey across the desert in a field ambulance did not exactly enhance the situation. He was flown to South Africa for treatment and eventually arrived home in 1943 with a 'stiff starboard leg', but such was his zest for life that his friend Herbie carried him down to the river where he pursued his hobby of fishing. The years passed and he mastered the inconvenience of his war wound to such an extent that he was once again out on the rocks in Snowdonia and actually leading on the famous wall climb on Tryfan to say nothing of Lockwood's Chimney.

In 1949, as a result of an advert in the Liverpool Echo, he found what was to be his pride and joy- a Mylne boat with a cabin. He surveyed her in Scotland and after an horrendous trip back to the Mersey from the Clyde he named her 'Dolphin'.

Over the next 25 years he raced her, sailed her hard and won most of the cups in the area. Every year there was a pilgrimage to Scotland and Ireland with different crews and it is safe to say that no single yacht has given so many people so much pleasure over so many years. We all respected him for his seamanship and judgement and turned to him for advice and counsel, which he always readily gave. He was a friend to all; everyone from Tobermory to Portmadoc, where he crewed on the Lifeboats, knew John Ivory and the by now famous exploits of Dolphin.

I could fill a book with the events that can be linked with this man. During the latter years his terrible war wounds started to take their toll. With his natural zest for life and outdoor activities being curtailed he was forced gradually to withdraw from the world, the people and the pursuits he loved and enjoyed so much. I will conclude with one of Joni's sayings, "Be of good cheer, tight lines to the fishermen and always keep a windward berth for the yachtsmen."

A few days after the funeral, Vicki came with me to sort out the contents of Joni's flat in Wallasey. We knew he had very little but we had to see that his bequests were attended to. He had left all Dolphin's Logs to his sailing friends and various pieces of china, rugs etc to the family. It was heartbreaking, but Vicki kept my spirits up and made me laugh at one time. The flat had to be completely cleared and we had sent a few things to a sale room and what was left went to a house clearance firm. But when we opened a door in the top attic and found it full of junk, Vicki locked the door and threw the key out of the window!

My last memory was of the little Jamie sitting on the bedroom floor with a blissful expression on his face, inspecting two little aluminium fly cases which I said he could keep.

* * * * *

Mr Roger Lancelyn Green of Poulton Hall in Wirral contacted NADFAS to enquire if any of the members would be prepared to restore all the books in the ancient library which had not been catalogued or professionally cleaned. Four of us; Francis Wise, Jean Forster, Mary Baldwin and myself, who had all worked at the cathedral library, were thrilled with the opportunity and volunteered at once.

On the first day we were due to arrive at the house, the four of us turned off the road to Raby Mere and approached the house through a tunnel of trees. The 18th century house had a handsome portico and long French windows. We rang the bell and the door was immediately opened by Scirard Lancelyn Green who welcomed us and conducted us to the Organ Room which was once the Billiard Room where we met the other 'Library girls'. There, too, was the rest of the family including their two little boys Randal aged 7 and Arthur aged 4. They were all so welcoming and made us feel, in the true sense of the words, like part of the family.

The family has lived on the estate for nearly a

thousand years, farming the land. Their first home was a castle of which there are now no visible remains. The present house is a series of buildings spreading back from the porticoed white house to ivy covered buildings at the rear, overlooking a courtyard. There is a kitchen garden and a walled garden. The façade of the main building, built in brick, has been pebble-dashed and white washed. At the rear of the house is the range of farm buildings.

We again met Caroline who had trained us at the Chester Cathedral Library and was to give us a refresher course. I was fascinated with the contents of the Organ Room as the walls were covered with trophies from all over the world. After introductions all round, we were left with Caroline who took us through the procedure of cleaning and repairing the books once more. Scirard Lancelyn Green then returned and, after handing us a glass of sherry, invited us all to follow him to the dining room where we were invited to help ourselves to the many delicious home made dishes set before us.

The work of cleaning the books was divided between sixteen of us, who worked a day each week, bringing our own picnic lunch.

We entered from the front door into a dark panelled hall, the walls of which are covered with a rich William Morris wallpaper. At one side of the hall stands a life size bear and on a table at the foot of the stairs is the largest gong I have ever seen, made of first world war brass shell cases. The hall and staircase are covered with a rich red carpet on which we were delighted to see the children's toys scattered about. Scirard's petite wife Caroline took us upstairs through a white painted corridor on whose walls were family portraits and many intriguing little wall cupboards. On up again to a small room at the top of the house which was to be our work room and was the Upper Library, once known as the Muniment Room. Every inch of the walls was covered with glass covered shelves packed with mostly cloth-covered books. There was a large table surrounded by comfortable chairs and a stove. Where there were no books, a desk and the mantelpiece were covered with family treasures.

We loved our room from the very beginning. All the materials we needed for working on the books were provided and by now we knew exactly what was needed. In the ceiling above the table was a large skylight, which was a cause of much hilarity, as from time to time water dripped through so there was a rush to protect the valuable books in our care.

Then Mrs Lancelyn Green took us downstairs to the main library to collect our books. The room was intimate and breathtaking. Built by Thomas Green, Lord of the Manor of Poulton and Lower Bebington and Rector of Woodchurch in the 18th century, the room is panelled in carved pine, now a rich golden brown, that forms a series of arches, the books packed in the shelves in recessed bays.

Rows of leather bound books were in shelves along one wall. An enormous armchair, packed with many cushions, stood in one corner near a desk. On the wide windowsills and many small tables round the room was a collection of porcelain, copper and bronze which jostled in a kind of careless abandon.

We each collected an armful of books and returned to our workroom. As the majority of the books were 18th century, the leather needed careful treatment with a special leather dressing. Frayed and torn corners were stuck back in position and the books bandaged until set. They were then carefully buffed up with a soft duster. Every page of the book was cleaned with a soft brush and we looked for any sign of insect damage or tears.

In so doing, we often digressed and started to read the text describing old family accounts, recipes and instructions for the daily duties of servants, indoors and out, giving an insight into the 18th century family life of a farming squire. Every book then had its own docket in which is recorded the author's name, title, date of publication, shelf number, book number and if there was any damage or missing pages.

Sadly, all good things come to an end but the Lancelyn Greens did not let us go without entertaining us all to a delicious lunch in the Garden Room and a magic lantern talk on the old house given by Mrs June Lancelyn Green.

* * * * *

And then it happened. Since my last eye operation I had dreaded the moment when the retina in the other eye became detached. Although it was always in the back of my mind, I filled my days so that I had as little time as possible to think about it.

I came down to breakfast and I could see a black area blotting out part of my sight, so I rang my doctor and told him what had happened. He came up to see me in a quarter of an hour, examined my eye and said, "*I'm afraid it is a detached retina. You will have to have it attended to at once*". He rang Mr Armstrong, the local eye specialist, but he was away. "*I will get in touch with Mr Wong at Heswall to book you in to Murrayfield tomorrow morning*". I rang my friend Doreen who lived only a mile away from the Hospital to tell her what had happened and she promised to visit me there as Martin and Jenny and the children were off to Abersoch that weekend.

At 9.30 the following morning my doctor rang to say Mr. Wong was also away, so I had to report to St. Paul's Eye Hospital that morning at 10.30. I was all on my own as Jenny had been on duty the night before at a local Nursing Home and was in bed sleeping. Martin had left early to go to Garstang on the other side of Cheshire and I had no way of contacting him so, as I could hardly see, I rang some friends to see if they could take me to hospital but without success.

I then thought of my friend Doreen in Heswall and told her I was not going to Murrayfield after all but to St. Paul's Eye Hospital in Liverpool and that as Martin and Jenny were unavailable I asked if she could possibly run me over. *"I'll come at once,"* she replied. I don't know when I have felt so grateful. It was always a joy to see her anyway with her shiny good health and mop of tight curly hair. She arrived about three quarters of an hour later and we drove through the tunnel to St. Paul's Eye Hospital in Liverpool. It is not an easy building to find and when you get there its very enormity fills you with dread. It has, to me, the appearance of a prison. With dragging steps I followed Doreen to the reception desk in the very impersonal waiting area.

After my previous admission to the Chester Royal Infirmary for the same operation, where the nurses were dressed in pale pink and blue dresses with starched white aprons, the staff here did not fill me with any confidence dressed as they were, all alike, in dull navy overalls and black stockings and shoes, which I found very depressing.

As I was going to be here for a long time, I told Doreen not to wait. I had rung Vicki in Hampshire before I left, begging her to come as soon as possible. She was off to Abersoch with Martin and Jenny in three days but she promised to come at once.

After the usual tests that have to be done before any operation I met my surgeon who was a South African. I told him the trouble I had had with my last anaesthetic and that the correct mix for me was on record at the Nuffield Hospital in Chester. Although I frequently asked at reception if they had heard from the Nuffield, it was 6 o'clock in the evening before the nurse told me that they had the information. I was then taken to a ward which had no other occupants.

I was sitting on the edge of the bed, lonely and depressed, when suddenly the door opened and in rushed Vicki, who flung her arms around me. An hour later I went down to theatre. The operation was a success and within hours, though totally blind. I was advised to walk about all day as much as possible. Frankly, I remember very little about the day and a half in hospital before I was discharged. Weak and unable to see, I don't remember even getting in and out of bed, I only knew that Vicki was there to hold my hand and encourage me. The next day we returned home and the following day Doreen took me home with her whilst Vicki, Martin and Jenny went to Abersoch. The surgeon flew back to South Africa the day after the operation.

Weeks and weeks of drops three times a day gradually restored my partial sight, but without Doreen's care and companionship, my early days of blindness would have been much slower. Without her I was helpless. How much I owed to her friendship. I shall never cease to be grateful to my old friend.

A few years ago Martin decided to cut down all the

non-bearing apple trees in the centre of the orchard. This opened up a glorious vista to the fields, sky and woods at the end of our garden with only an open wire fence between.

From my conservatory I have an uninterrupted view of the cows in the farmer's field and the squirrels, rabbits, pigeons and wild birds that inhabit the fields and woods around our garden. There is no sound of the traffic from the main road at the front of our house. In spring there are drifts of snowdrops followed by hundreds of daffodils and all the fruit blossom of the pear, apple and damson trees. It is utterly peaceful. The colours in the trees and distant woods continually change, not only with the seasons of the year, but with the hours of daylight and sunshine. In spring the trees in the woods are a deep violet in the shadow with soft brown branches and the stubble field quite pink.

The field adjoining our garden is a very old meadow. The ridge and furrow markings can still be seen when the rays of the setting sun slant across it and the cattle come up.

Today when the world is obsessed with Peps and the Lottery, I am glad that I do not have to depend on them, for the best things in life are free. A wood full of bluebells, primroses in a lane, a friend's smile, the feel of a warm egg taken from a hen's nest, the cry of the curlew, a letter from a granddaughter upon receiving her 21st birthday present, *"To my dearest, darling Grandmother. Thank you so much for my birthday present. You were silly saying they weren't very good - Granny they were the most thoughtful, meaningful presents that I was given and I will treasure them for ever. I love you so dearly."*

You cannot buy these things. They are beyond price.

Other books by Joan Rocke;

"A Wirral Childhood" £2.95

A5 - 44pp - This is a series of stories of her childhood from her earliest memories to her early teens.

Published by Joan Rocke - Recently reprinted

Other books by Classfern Ltd;

"Wirral Memories" £6.95

A4 - 100pp - Full gloss colour compilation of nostalgic articles about Wirral, its people and its places, written by the editor of and contributors to Wirral Champion Magazine.

"Wheelchair Pilot" £9.95

A4 - 100pp - Full gloss colour chronicle of the extraordinary exploits, the writings and the cartoons of Swasie Turner, an invalided policeman who subsequently lost his leg and has become a champion of disabled charities. Written by John M Birtwistle, Editor/Publisher of Wirral Champion Magazine.

Both books available in bookshops and by mail-order from publisher, tel; 0151 608 6333.